NO LONGER SHACKLED

BREAKING FREE OF SIN'S CONTROL

By Mark Garver

All scripture is quoted from The King James Version of the Bible unless otherwise noted.

Scripture quotations marked (KJV) are taken from *The King James Version*. Copyright © 1979, 1980, 1982, Thomas Nelson, Inc.

Scripture quotations marked (NKJV) are taken from the *New King James Version*. Copyright © 1982 by Thomas Nelson, Inc. Used by permission. All rights reserved.

Scripture quotations marked (The Message) are taken from *The Message*. Copyright © 1993, 1994, 1995, 1996, 2000, 2001, 2002. Used by permission of NavPress Publishing Group.

Scripture quotations marked (NLT) are taken from the *Holy Bible, New Living Translation*, copyright © 1996, 2004, 2007 by Tyndale House Foundation. Used by permission of Tyndale House Publishers, Inc., Carol Stream, Illinois 60188. All rights reserved.

Scripture quotations marked (AMP) are taken from the *Amplified® Bible*, Copyright © 1954, 1958, 1962, 1964, 1965, 1987 by The Lockman Foundation. Used by permission. (www.Lockman.org)

Scripture quotations marked (Phillips) are taken from The New Testament in Modern English, (Rev. Ed.) by J.B. Phillips. Copyright © 1958, 1960, 1972 by J.B. Phillips. Reprinted by permission of Macmillan Publishing Co., New York, New York.

Scripture quotations marked (NAS) are taken from *The New American Standard Bible*. Copyright © the Lockman Foundation 1960, 1962, 1963, 1968, 1971, 1972, 1973, 1975, 1977. Used by permission.

Rick Renner, *Sparking Gems from the Greek;* Teach All Nations, a division of Rick Renner Ministries, Tulsa, OK. Copyright © 2003. Used by permission.

Rick Renner, *Dressed to Kill;* Teach All Nations, a division of Rick Renner Ministries, Tulsa, OK.. Copyright © 1991, New edition 2007. Used by permission.

NO LONGER SHACKLED
Breaking Free of Sin's Control
978-0-9891429-0-8

Published by Mountz Media & Publishing
Tulsa, Oklahoma 74170-2398
918.296.0995
www.mountzmedia.com

Copyright © 2013 by Mark Garver. Printed in the United States of America. All rights reserved under International Copyright Law. Contents and/or cover may not be reproduced in whole or in part in any form without the express written consent of the author and publisher.

CONTENTS

CHAPTER 1 5
BREAKING FREE OF SIN

CHAPTER 2 15
THE TRUTH ABOUT TEMPTATION

CHAPTER 3 35
MY FLESH! MY FLESH!

CHAPTER 4 61
AN ESCAPE THEOLOGY

CHAPTER 5 79
YOU'RE THE BOSS

CHAPTER 6 95
WALK IN THE SPIRIT AND AWAY FROM SIN

CHAPTER 7 107
THE BENEFITS OF RIGHTEOUSNESS

CHAPTER 8 117
THE MIND IS A TERRIBLE THING TO WASTE

CHAPTER 9 135
A MULTIPLAN ATTACK ON SIN

CHAPTER 10 147
LIVING FREE

CHAPTER 1
BREAKING FREE OF SIN

We all deal with sin. It's our enemy, and it's everywhere. It comes to every one of us—believers and unbelievers alike—and traps us in a life we do not want. In fact, the Bible guarantees that we will confront temptation and sin. So it's not *if* sin will come to us, but what we'll do *when* it comes.

You might think this only applies to sexual sins or sins that most folks consider really bad. But that's not true. Sin is sin, and all sin leads to bondage.

People in sin need help getting free because it's almost as if someone came along and chained them, tied them up or shackled them. Their hands and feet are bound even though they struggle with all their strength to get free. Their only salvation would be if someone came and released them.

Someone did.

That's exactly what Jesus has done for us; He loosed us from the chains that bound us, and now we are *no longer shackled.*

Jesus set you free and loosed you from every evil force of darkness that tries to hold you captive. That means the only thing that can keep you bound is *you*. To walk in freedom, you must receive all that Jesus has provided for you and be convinced of your freedom. The Word of God does the convincing, so don't take my word for it. Take God's word for it; take God *at His Word*.

Let's look at what the Bible says about walking free of bondage. God makes it clear throughout the Bible that in order for His promises to belong to us, we must believe them and receive them as our own. So let's take hold of His Word together that promises us freedom from sin.

GOD SAYS YOU'RE FREE

The first step to receive from God is to know His will in the matter. Some people think that it's hard to know the will of God, but that's just not true. Knowing God's will is easy once you know what the Bible has to say because the Word of God *is* the will of God.

In other words, if we want to know God's will in a matter, we need to check out what the Bible says. The Bible is 66 books of God's thoughts and ways; it's God talking to us. God's Word is a manual or a guidebook written to tell us how to live successfully on this earth. The Holy Spirit supernaturally moved on men of old to write the Bible, and every word it contains is quick, alive and full of the power to bring itself to pass (Hebrews 4:12). It's no ordinary book; it's God talking directly to you and me.

"But if God's will is His Word, then what difference does it make if I believe it?" someone might ask. The answer is simple: The will of God is not automatically accomplished in our lives simply because it's His will. If that were true, then everyone would be born again because the Bible says that it's not God's will that anyone should perish or be lost, but all should receive salvation (2 Peter 3:9). Yet, unfortunately, people die every day without ever knowing Jesus.

The bottom line is that even though God's will is stated in His Word, you and I must choose whether or not we will believe His Word. If we choose to believe God's promises, then our faith in God's Word brings His promises to pass in our lives.

Let's talk for a minute about God's will in the area of freedom from sin. Does God want you free from sin? Free from habits? Free from whatever trips you up and binds you? Or does God send sin and temptation to test you and make you a better and a stronger person?

God's Word has the answers. Psalm 91:3 says, "Surely He shall deliver you from the snare of the fowler and from the perilous pestilence" (NKJV). Does this scripture say that maybe or sometimes God will deliver you? No. It says *surely*—*absolutely without a doubt*—God will deliver you. It's a definite thing, a promise.

So from what will He deliver us? Verse 3 said He will deliver us from the "snare of the fowler," or from every trap the enemy sets. What is the biggest trap of the enemy? Sin!

It doesn't matter how long you've been trapped or held captive by sin. It doesn't matter how long you have dealt with a particular sin, and it doesn't matter what kind of sin it is. God doesn't rate sin on a 1-10 scale from bad to worse like some people do. God just promises to deliver you from every sin if you will follow Him.

It's important to understand that sin is not your cross to bear. God wants you free from anything and everything that binds you. Sadly, I've heard people mistakenly say that some of us have sins to bear since we're supposed to take up our cross and follow Jesus. But your cross to bear is not sin. Your cross to bear is nothing from which Jesus already redeemed you. Your cross to bear is simply laying down your way of doing things and picking up His way of doing things.

In the following chapters we'll talk more about how sin is a twofold problem that involves the devil and your human flesh. Either way, God sent Jesus to deliver you from things that have happened in your past, things that hold you in bondage and things that make you think wrong and act wrong. God wants you completely delivered from any bad habits and all sins.

The Bible says that Jesus came to give us abundant life, which is a good and satisfying life. He wants you to have a good marriage and a good family life. God wants you to do well at your job; He wants you to succeed. If you're dealing with a bad habit, God wants you delivered. If you've wrestled with depression or oppression, God wants you set free. If you've struggled with bondage in any area of your life, God wants you free.

Maybe you cannot keep a job, and you think the last six bosses didn't understand you. Maybe you continually go from relationship to relationship. In both these situations, the common denominator is you, so maybe you need to be delivered from you. You need some things fixed in your life, and God will do it. God promises He will deliver you.

Maybe you've been a Christian a long time, but you fell into sin. God will deliver you. Maybe you were a minister who made a mistake and got into sin; God will deliver you. Maybe you were born again yesterday, but sinned today; God will deliver you. Maybe you aren't born again at all; God will deliver you if you will turn to Him. No matter your circumstances, God wants to help you and free you from the shackles that have put you in bondage.

James 1:17 says, "Every good gift and every perfect gift . . . comes down from the Father . . ." (NKJV). Ephesians 2:10 in The Amplified Bible says that God has prearranged a plan that you walk in the good life. God is good and He wants only good for us. So begin to put God's goodness to work right now and say aloud with me, "God will deliver me out of the snare of the fowler or the trapper. God will deliver me out of the devil's hands. God will deliver me from myself if that's what it takes."

Let's look at another promise of deliverance from the Word of God. Second Timothy 4:18 says, "The Lord will deliver me from every evil work, and will preserve me unto his heavenly kingdom: to whom be glory for ever and ever. Amen." Isn't that good? Again, God promises to deliver you or free you from every evil work. No matter what fleshly temptation the devil has used to entice you, God has given you a get out of jail free card. Did you hear me? God has said that He would get you out of bondage and deliver you from every evil work.

Think about that! God not only promises to get you out of sin, but He also promises you something even better. God says He has set you into the heavenly kingdom, which means you get to start living like a king right now on the earth.

Second Peter 2:9 says, "The Lord knows how to deliver the godly out of temptations...." (NKJV). Aren't you glad God knows how to deliver you? Aren't you happy to know that you're not stuck in sin? God has provided a way out of temptations; He's provided the escape to freedom. You may not know how to get out of trouble and stay out of trouble, but God does. He's made a way for you to be free from the sin that tracks you like a dog tracks a raccoon.

TREED BY THE DEVIL

Back in Illinois, where I'm from originally, my dad would go raccoon hunting with his coon dog named Bud. I know that sounds like some make believe detail from a movie, but it's the truth. The example also makes a real point about how the devil likes to harass Christians.

My dad would start out hunting and turn Bud loose in the woods to pick up the scent of a raccoon. While Bud was on the trail, he would let out a certain bark to let Dad know he had found a raccoon. Then suddenly Bud's bark would change and my dad would know that Bud had treed that raccoon. *Treed* is a hunting term used to describe how Bud had trapped the raccoon up a tree, where it had no way of escape and was about to meet a bullet and become a fur hat.

In the same way, the devil tries to trap Christians so they feel treed. Maybe you feel bound by sin and habits with no way out, feeling like your life is over. Here's the good news: You are no raccoon, and you don't have to stay bound. There is a way out. God knows how to deliver you out of every temptation the devil can throw at you. But the first step toward freedom is you believing you can be free. God needs you to do that. God needs you to believe that He has delivered you from every evil work and every evil trap the devil has set for you.

Do you believe Him? Do you accept what God has said? If so, begin to say aloud, "I don't want to sin, and I don't have to sin."

GO AND SIN NO MORE

Jesus once told a woman that she didn't have to sin anymore, and it changed her life. We read about this woman who had committed adultery in John 8. She was caught in sin and publicly brought to Jesus by religious leaders. Trying to test Jesus, these angry accusers reminded Him that Moses' law required the woman to be stoned and then asked Him what He had to say about her sin.

Jesus told them that whomever was without sin in the group should cast the first stone. One by one the accusers left without saying a word. Then when Jesus was alone with the woman He asked her, "Woman, where are those accusers of yours? Has no one condemned you?" (verse10).

"No one, Lord," she said (verse 11).

"Neither do I condemn you; go and sin no more," Jesus said (verse 11).

Those are powerful words Jesus spoke. In fact, when He said "Go and sin no more" to the woman, I believe He was speaking to us also. I believe Jesus was and is saying to every one of us today: Neither do I condemn you for your sin, but go and sin no more. I believe that Jesus was communicating heaven's desire for each and every one of us, and I believe He was also making sure that we understand that it's possible to live a life free of sin.

You can go and sin no more.

God doesn't want you tied to things that hold you down or hold you captive. God wants you free from anything and everything that binds you, no matter how big or how small it is.

GUILT AND CONDEMNATION

Just as much as God wants you free of sin, He also wants you free of the guilt sin causes. God doesn't want you to live in condemnation. He didn't set you free from sin so you could continually worry about your former lifestyle of sin and carry the baggage of guilt everywhere you go. No, when God sets you free, you are free indeed.

In the encounter between Jesus and the woman in John 8, you'll recall that Jesus did not condemn the woman, and He is not condemning you and me. After we've repented and God has forgiven our sins, condemnation should not be anywhere near us. Romans 8:1 says, "There is therefore now no condemnation to those who are in Christ Jesus, who do not walk according to the flesh, but according to the Spirit" (NKJV).

If you are feeling convicted, that's something entirely different. There's a big difference between conviction and condemnation. When you're living in sin and the Spirit of God deals with you to change an area of your life or He points out and highlights sin in your life, that's conviction. You should actually be happy when you feel convicted. That's the Holy Spirit talking to you; He's trying to help you. So when you feel convicted, deal with the conviction immediately; ask for forgiveness and make a change.

Condemnation, on the other hand, is a feeling of guilt, and it never comes from God. What did Jesus say to the woman caught in adultery? Did He say He condemned her? No. Jesus said, "Neither do I condemn you." Condemnation never comes from God; Jesus bore your guilt and your shame. Condemnation always comes from the devil, and it comes from religious people who try to make you feel guilty and unworthy.

Let me put it this way. Conviction is when the Holy Ghost says, "Stop it! Don't do that! That will pull you away from the Father." Condemnation is when you think, "I feel guilty. I feel ashamed. I'm just a rotten worm. I'm just a sinner." But if you're born again, you're no longer a sinner; you have received God's amazing grace and you have become a child of God, a joint heir with Jesus. You have royal blood flowing through your veins; you've got the DNA of God Almighty on the inside of you because you're a new creature in Christ Jesus.

If you've accepted Jesus Christ as your Lord and Savior—and if you've asked God to forgive you of your sin—He has forgiven and forgotten your sins. The Bible says when God forgives He forgets, and your sins are as far as the east is from the west (Psalm 103:12). If you have not yet received Jesus as your Lord and Savior, you're probably dealing with sin morning, noon and night. But your life can turn around in an instant, so don't tolerate guilt and condemnation for another minute. *(If you have not made Jesus the Lord of your life, turn to page 165 and pray a prayer that will change your life forever.)*

Religion sometimes likes to tell people that guilt and condemnation are good, but that's a lie. Condemnation will separate you from God—and there's nothing worse than that. If you feel condemned about sin, you won't go boldly into God's presence where you can receive help in time of need.

GET SMART

Whether you've never met Jesus Christ, you're newly born again or you've been in the family of God for 30 years, you will never grow past temptation and sin. As long as you are alive on this earth, you'll have the opportunity to resist sin.

In fact, it's so important for us to be aware that sin comes to all because if we let our guard down, the devil will be right there to put us into bondage. When we think we're smarter than the devil or we think we don't need to keep our flesh under, we set ourselves up for a big fall. It's called pride, and it comes before destruction.

No matter whether you've had an occasional problem with sin, a regular problem with sin or you don't think you have trouble with sin at all, this message is still for you. If you live in a body and live on this earth, this message is for you. If you want to live in victory—healthy, wealthy and wise—this message is for you.

The most important question becomes: How can we get free from sin and stay free from sin? The Bible has all the answers to this question and more, which we'll look at in the chapters to come.

CHAPTER 2
THE TRUTH ABOUT TEMPTATION

The more we understand what sin is all about and how it works, the better equipped we are to break free from its control. Actually, people usually don't like to talk about sin, and yet, understanding how it works gives us the advantage and the power to get free from it. Turning on the lights always chases away the darkness.

Let's begin to consider the truth about sin by asking ourselves some important questions on the topic and then searching God's Word to find the answers. Where does sin come from? Is sin God's way of testing us? How does sin work? Best yet, how can we stay away from sin altogether?

THE ORIGIN OF SIN

Many people believe God uses sin, temptation and the evils of this world to test us, but that's not the case. The Bible clearly tells us where sin, temptation and evil do and don't come from, so let's be clear that they don't come from God.

Temptation and sin never come from God. It's important to be rock solid on this truth because if we don't know the origin of something, we don't know who or what we're fighting against or resisting. We know that we shouldn't fight against God, but since many people think the temptation to sin comes from God as a test, they're not sure whether to roll over and accept it or resist it. They change their voices and go all King James-sounding, saying, "Mine heart is saddened that I have fallen into sin and failed the test that God sendeth me." That may sound reasonable and religious, but it's still wrong.

We can resolve this once and for all from the Word of God. James 1:13 says, "Let no one say when he is tempted, 'I am tempted by God'; for God cannot be tempted by evil, nor does He Himself tempt anyone." Then 1 Thessalonians 3:5 says, "For this reason, when I could no longer endure it, I sent to know your faith, lest by some means *the tempter had tempted you*, and our labor might be in vain" (NKJV). Who tempts you? The devil is the tempter.

God has never tempted your flesh to sin, but the devil has been tempting you as far back as you can remember. Did you get that? Temptation to sin only comes from one source: the devil. Period. That's right. The devil is the "bad boy" who does the tempting.

Notice how James teaches us on the topic.

> **James 1:12-15 (NKJV)**
> 12 Blessed *is* the man who endures temptation; for when he has been approved, he will receive the crown of life which the Lord has promised to those who love Him.
>
> 13 Let no one say when he is tempted, "I am tempted by God"; for God cannot be tempted by evil, nor does He Himself tempt anyone.
>
> 14 But each one is tempted when he is

> drawn away by his own desires [lusts] and enticed.
>
> 15 Then, when desire has conceived, it gives birth to sin; and sin, when it is full-grown, brings forth death.

Did James say that God tests us with temptation and sin? No. He said the exact opposite. What did we just read in James 1:13? It said, "Let no one say when he is tempted, 'I am tempted of God.'" James went on to tell us that "God cannot be tempted with evil, nor does He Himself tempt anyone."

Verse 14 gave us even more detail and said, "…Each one is tempted when he is drawn away by his own desires [or lust] and enticed." Notice that last phrase again, "when he is drawn away of his own lust and enticed." We will talk about lust and enticement later because it has much to do with sinning and not sinning. But again, who does the tempting and entices us? First Thessalonians 3:5 said it was the devil. He's the culprit. The title of tempter belongs to the devil, and he tempts you every time he can get by with it and every which way he can; the devil downright coaxes you to sin and probably does a happy dance if we fall for his plan.

Let's look at a few more scriptures where the Bible clearly identifies the devil as the tempter. Matthew 4:3, "Now *when the tempter came to Him*, he said, 'If You are the Son of God, command that these stones become bread'"(NKJV). Second Corinthians 11:3 says, "But I fear, lest by any means, as the *serpent beguiled* Eve through his subtlety, so your minds should be corrupted from the simplicity that is in Christ."

Who was the serpent? The devil. Clearly, it's not God who tempts us, but the devil. God is not the tempter, and He doesn't tempt you in anyway, anywhere or anytime. Recognize that temptation and sin are weapons of the devil to trick you, defeat you and get you off track. Refuse to let him influence you.

TEST OR TEMPTATION

Even after some folks become convinced that God will not tempt them, they begin to ask if God will test them. Yet, there is a very big difference between a test and a temptation. A test can come from God, but a temptation will never come from God. Even more importantly, a temptation is never a test.

People sometimes struggle to find the line between a temptation and a test, but think about these examples for a minute.

Guys, let's say a woman walks by you in a string bikini; it's not a test from God to see if you can maintain pure thoughts. It's not a test to see how well your eyesight functions or anything like that. Women, if a guy walks by shirtless showing his tanned, rippled abs and huge pecs, it's not a test to see if you can keep your mind focused on the Lord or keep your mind focused on your husband. It's not a test to see how disciplined your mind is.

Along this same line, if you were delivered from alcohol, God doesn't send one of your buddies by your house with a six-pack to see how you're doing. That would be the devil. That's not how God tests you.

You may be laughing as you think about these examples, but a lot of people struggle to understand that God is not the tempter. God does not steal, kill or destroy (John 10:10). He doesn't steal our health. He doesn't steal our money, and He doesn't send trouble our way. God sent Jesus to give His children abundant life, and anything that is not abundant life is not from God.

Consider this example. Let's say a man used to steal when he was a kid, but when he's much older he stands in front of an ATM that suddenly begins to spit out thousands of dollars that are not his. Is that God testing Him? No. Let's say an armored car travels down the street and the driver drops $10,000. Is that a test from God? No. God does not set you up for failure.

That's not how God tests us. But God will give us open book tests with His Word. In other words, God will check to see if we're obedient to His Word or if we follow the leadings and the promptings of the Holy Ghost. For instance, God says, "Will you obey me?" "How will you handle your money?" "Are you going to tithe?" That's how God tests us.

On the other side, as we saw in James 1, the devil very deliberately comes to tempt you. He's not playing around; the devil wants you to mess up and get in as much trouble as possible. He's out to ruin your life. Yet, the Bible says if you're born again that the devil is under your feet (Ephesians 1:22). You've been raised to sit in heavenly places with Christ Jesus (Ephesians 2:6). The Bible says that you don't have to be ignorant of the devil's devices (2 Corinthians 2:11). The Bible says you can win against the devil every time (2 Corinthians 2:14).

Therefore, when sin comes in front of you, you don't have to wonder, *Where does this come from?* When sin comes along, you'll be able to confidently know and say, "That's the work of the devil. That's the devil trying to get me out of the will of God. That's the devil trying to pull me away from my heavenly Father. That's the devil trying to pull me away from my family. That's the devil trying to ruin my life."

The devil doesn't come against us with a red suit and tail, horns and a pitch fork. How does the devil come? He comes with sin. Sickness. Confusion and every evil work. But I've got good news. First John 3:8 says, ". . . For this purpose the Son of God was manifested, that He might destroy the works of the devil" (NKJV).

You've got to clearly know that temptation is the work of the devil, and you've got to know there's a way out. When a temptation comes to a born-again believer, there's always a way out. You don't have to give into the temptation and commit a sin.

You also need to realize that the temptation is not the sin. Temptation first comes as a thought to disobey God and His Word, but that in and of itself is not sin. The sin comes when a person acts upon the thought. So don't act upon the thoughts of temptation; cut them off before they escalate.

Jesus Himself was tempted. Hebrews 2:18 says, "For in that he himself hath suffered being tempted, he is able to succour them that are tempted." The word *succour* means *to run to the cry of and assist and relieve* those who are tempted. The Bible also says in 2 Peter 2:9, "The Lord knows how to deliver the godly out of temptations . . ." (NKJV). Isn't that good news? If you find yourself tempted, there's help available. God has made a way out of all temptation, and He will deliver you out of them all if you'll follow Him.

YOUR PART OF THE EQUATION

We've established that the devil is responsible for introducing temptation and sin, but that's not the end of the story. James explained there's another element of the sin equation: *you*. James said that temptation comes because we are drawn away of our own lusts, and when lust is conceived, it produces sin.

That means the devil isn't the sum total of the sin problem; you're the other half of the problem. The devil may dangle temptation your way, but you choose whether to give in to sin or turn it down. But know this. The Bible arms you with insight into your enemy and gives you all the equipment you need to defeat the temptation and the devil.

God says that as Christians we are more than conquerors (Romans 8:37), and we can do all things through Jesus Christ who strengthens us (Philippians 4:13). So it's our job to understand the process of sin and walk in the freedom from sin that Jesus won for us.

THE PROCESS OF SIN

The first thing we need to understand about the process of sin is that sin doesn't just happen to us out of the blue one day. A person might feel that way. A person might feel shocked that he or she gave way to sin and feel like the trap of sin came out of nowhere, but the truth is, the act of sin developed over time. It was a process. One thought after another and one poor choice after another paved the way for the sin to overpower us.

You see, sin is a result of temptation, and every man, woman, boy and girl endures temptation; we all have to deal with some level of temptation all our lives. If we don't deal with the temptation when it first raises its ugly head and is small, then it's likely to grow beyond our ability to control it.

Notice again what God's Word has to say on the topic. James 1:14-15 says, "But *every man is tempted*, when he is *drawn away of his own lust, and enticed*. The scriptures go on to say that when lust has conceived it brings forth sin, and sin, when it is finished, brings forth death. Here's the devil's formula: temptation + lust = the conception of sin.

According to the Merriam-Webster Dictionary, the word *conceive* means "to become pregnant with, to take into one's mind, to cause to begin, to form and imagine in one's own mind." Do you see the pattern here? The devil dangles a well-chosen carrot of sin in front of a person to entice him or her, and then the person takes hold or becomes pregnant with the idea of something. The entire process of sin begins when a person takes an idea or thought or image into his or her mind and considers it, forms it, plays with it and imagines it.

As I was studying this subject a few years back, the word *conceive* seemed to jump off the page as I read this scripture; it gave me real insight. Notice James 1:14-15 again: "Every man is tempted, when he is drawn away of his own lust, and enticed. Then when lust hath conceived, it bringeth forth sin: and sin, when it is finished, bringeth forth death."

This word *conceive* highlights an important point: It takes two to tango. The process of sin is similar to the process of creating a baby. A man and a woman come together and conceive a child. It takes both the sperm and the egg. If the sperm and the egg don't come together, there will be no child. In the same way, the process of sin also requires two components—temptation and lust.

So, it's like this. We cannot control what the devil does. We cannot control when the devil comes. We cannot control that sin produces death. But we can control the lust of our flesh; without its participation, sin will not be conceived. Sin will be stopped in its tracks. It will be stopped cold.

Sin always begins with a single thought and continues to grow larger as it's fed with more thoughts and imaginations and eventually poor choices and actions. So let me clue you in here. The devil is after your mind and your body because that's where he does his dirty work to influence you. He wants to dominate your mind and your body, and he wants your spirit too weak to rise up and shut him down.

But we're going to put a stop to that. We're going to expose the tactics of your enemy and give away his strategies because if we can show you how he operates, you can refuse to cooperate with him. If you begin to realize how he operates, you'll be empowered to "go and sin no more."

To understand more about how he works, let me remind you that the Word of God explains that every human being is actually a three-part being. Each of us is a spirit who has a soul (mind, will and emotions) and lives in a body or suit of flesh. If you are born again, you believe in the resurrection of Jesus and have confessed Him as Lord; the Spirit of

God now lives within you, and when it comes to the devil, you're large and in charge as long as you follow God and obey His Word.

The devil has no authority over the born-again spirit where God dwells. If we walk in the freedom and authority we've been given, every shackle of sin drops off. We can break free from sin and no longer be ignorant of the devil's devices and schemes.

SIN: OLDER THAN ADAM AND EVE

The Bible says there's nothing new under the sun, which means the devil has been using the same old tricks since the beginning of time. He doesn't have any new devices or techniques. The devil doesn't have any new tricks; he just has new people to trick.

In fact, the devil tempted Eve's flesh in the same way he comes to tempt you and me. Now understand that Adam and Eve were made in the likeness and image of God, and they were totally alive to God. Before they fell to the temptation of sin, they were perfect because God made them perfect. But God also made them with a will of their own, and because of that free will, they fell to the temptation the devil brought to them.

"How could that happen?" someone might ask. "And what chance do we have if Adam and Eve couldn't withstand the temptation?" Again, we need to go to the Bible for the answers.

In the Garden of Eden, God had created the perfect setting. He made a beautiful and lush garden. We can look around the earth and see that God never does anything halfway. God Himself said everything He had made was good. I'm sure the skies were shimmering with light, the water was crystal clear and the fruit was bountiful and tasty.

Life was perfect for Adam and Eve. They lived in a paradise where God told them to enjoy themselves, and He fellowshipped with them regularly. God even put them in charge and told them to guard and protect the garden and to have dominion over every fowl in the air and beast that creeps on the ground. Really, God only gave Adam and Eve one command. He told them to enjoy everything about the garden except not to eat of one tree.

Then the devil showed up to tempt Eve with another idea. Second Corinthians 11:3 says, "...the serpent beguiled Eve through his subtilty...." Think about this. Adam and Eve had dominion and authority over the devil because they were given authority over every beast that creeps on the ground, but he cleverly came along to tempt Eve's resolve.

In Genesis 3:1-15, the Bible tells us about the encounter Eve had with her enemy and ours. As we look at this unfortunate first encounter with sin, keep in mind that the devil is playing the same game today. He reveals his strategies and tactics right here for all of mankind to see.

We learn that the devil is subtle. We learn that he's a good liar and deceiver. We learn that he makes sin look so enticing, but keep in mind that Jesus calls the devil the Father of Lies (John 8:44). So if the devil tells you that something is good, what does that really tell you?

We also learn that the devil likes to challenge the Word of God. That's the trick he pulled on Eve. The Amplified Bible says, "Now the serpent was more subtle and crafty than any living creature of the field which the Lord God had made. And he [Satan] said to the woman, *Can it really be that God has said, 'You shall not eat from every tree of the garden?'*" (Genesis 3:1). Think about his technique then and think about his technique now. He took his first shot trying to get Eve off the Word. He wanted her to question the Word and disagree with it. Doesn't he try the same with you?

Hasn't the devil said to you about God's Word, "Can it really be that God said...? Would it really be so bad if you...? Would it really hurt you to sin just this once? Who will know?" What a liar. God will know for One and you for another—and everyone else eventually.

Looking to pull Eve away from God's Word and out of obedience, the devil questioned Eve to see what she knew about the trees in the garden. The devil knows the Word of God, too, even though he misquotes it a lot. "…The woman said unto the serpent, We may eat of the fruit of the trees of the garden: But of the fruit of the tree which is in the midst of the garden, God hath said, Ye shall not eat of it, neither shall ye touch it, lest ye die" (Genesis 3:2-3).

Immediately the devil challenged the Word and Eve's knowledge of the Word by saying, "You won't die!" (NLT). That was only half true, and the devil is good at half truths. The whole truth is that by eating the fruit, Adam and Eve would not physically die, but they would spiritually die or be separated from God.

The devil's next trick was to put a first-class spin on sin, and Eve wasn't able to pass it up. The devil was trying to convince Eve that God was holding back on them. It's stupid when we think about it now, but the devil was working hard to push all Eve's buttons. He's slick, isn't he? He tried to convince Eve that God was deceiving her and withholding from them everything they needed to be all that they could be.

In verses 4-5 the devil says to Eve, "You won't die! . . . God knows that your eyes will be opened as soon as you eat it, and you will be like God, knowing both good and evil" (NLT). Can you believe it? The devil convinced Eve that she and Adam had not "arrived" and it was God's fault. Adam and Eve were not as "large and in charge" as they could or should be. He convinced her they would be as gods if they would eat the forbidden fruit.

The most interesting thing is that in reality Adam and Eve were already "gods" of this world because God had given them charge and authority over the whole earth. Doesn't this sound familiar? Isn't this tactic so like the devil? When he entices you with sin, he always tries to convince you that you're missing out on something and usually it's something you already have access to or have.

In reality the Word of God tells us that all the promises of God belong to us, and they are yes and amen (2 Corinthians 1:20). God is not withholding any good thing from them who walk uprightly (Psalm 84:11). God is not withholding from you. Everything He has is yours if you're His child. If he doesn't have it, He can make it. The only thing God cannot do is lie; He's bound Himself to keep His Word (Numbers 23:19).

But sure enough, Eve's flesh began to rare up and cause problems. In the next few sentences, you can see the whole process of temptation and sin for all mankind flash before your eyes. This verse makes it plain for all to see. "When the woman saw that the tree was good for food, and that it was pleasant to the eyes, and a tree to be desired to make one wise, she took of the fruit thereof, and did eat, and gave also unto her husband with her; and he did eat" (Genesis 3:6).

What we have here is the devil's foremost strategy in a nutshell. The devil targeted three things in Eve: the lust of the flesh, the lust of the eyes and the pride of life. You'll see those categories of sin over and over again in the Word of God, and you'll see those temptations over and over again in your life.

THREE CATEGORIES OF TEMPTATION

The Holy Spirit, through the apostle John, warns us about these same categories of temptation in 1 John. John lays out here the categorical devices the devil used against Eve to ensure the fall of mankind. The devil not only targeted Eve with these things, but he also targeted Jesus Himself. Think about it. If the devil goes after the "big dogs" in the Bible, do you think he'll try the same thing on you and me?

Let's look at 1 John 2:

1 John 2:15-16
15 Love not the world, neither the things that are in the world. If any man love the world, the love of the Father is not in him.

16 For all that is in the world, the **lust of the flesh**, and **the lust of the eyes**, and **the pride of life**, is not of the Father, but is of the world.

The **lust of the flesh** deals with the appetites of the flesh, our five senses and bodily cravings. In Eve's case it was the appeal of the fruit as good for food that had her mouth watering. She had to have it literally—at any cost. Does your flesh tell you that you have to have something? What appetites does the devil stir in you until it about drives you crazy and you feel like you just have to give in? Identify your weakness, so you can shore up your resolve.

Adam and Eve were perfectly created in the likeness and image of God, and there was no sin, no flaw in them. The problem is that there was a serpent in the Garden of Eden—a mouthy serpent—who understood that getting a child of God to entertain lust opens the door to sin.

The next category is the **lust of the eyes**. The food was pleasant to Eve's eyes, which is a big problem because the eyes are the window to the soul. The devil will always bring temptations before your eyes—in real time, in pictures of the past and even in imaginations of what could be. Unfortunately, there are even times when we cannot help what our eyes see; the devil makes sure that things pass before us. That's why we must keep our eyes focused on God's Word.

In other words, Eve craved something she was not supposed to have. She craved something that was bad for her, something that would eventually destroy her. I'm sure you've noticed that the flesh works that way, always wanting what it should not have.

There was a plethora of food to choose from in the garden, but naturally Eve wanted the one thing God told them not to eat. Why? "…It was pleasant to the eyes…" (verse 6). The lust of the eyes had taken hold. The eyes love to look at things they should not, and the devil loves to tempt us with things to see. If the devil can get us to look at things we should not see, then he has access to our soul realms where sin ignites.

This is true for men and women. Too often people think it's only a male problem, but that's not true. The lust of the eyes is a human problem, and we all need to be careful what we see. That's why the Lord tells us to meditate on the Word day and night and keep it before our eyes. What we see is important. When you think about it, we could lust after just about anything we can see from a new BMW to coconut cream pie. It doesn't matter what we're lusting after, lust is wrong. It's not godly, but it is deadly.

In case you haven't noticed, the devil likes to play the "sex card" on a pretty regular basis by tempting men and women with attractive members of the opposite sex. In teaching the men of our church, my wife, Rhonda, who pastors alongside me, often says, "Maybe you couldn't help the first look, but you sure can control the second, third and fourth looks." Unfortunately we sometimes turn those looks into stares, and it leads us right into sin. There's so much wisdom in her statement. In fact, if King David had understood that principle, he would not have gotten into a sinful relationship with Bathsheba (2 Samuel 11). Then again, I'm not just talking about sexual sins either. These basic categories of temptation are pathways the devil has developed for all kinds of sin.

The third category involves the **pride of life.** Eve saw that the tree would make her wise. In fact, the devil told her that she would be like a god. The pride of life tries to get us to elevate ourselves above others in our own strength. He wants us to make this life all about us.

As a pastor I see this all the time. I've watched the devil destroy people by convincing them that life is all about you, your wants, your needs, your desires, yourself. Bottom line, the pride of life is the devil getting you to think about *you*.

Notice how the devil's temptation strategy on Eve is something he knows about; it was his original sin. The devil thought he would elevate himself above God, and we all know how that turned out. Nevertheless, the devil would like for every one of us to adopt a prideful attitude that says, "I don't need God; I'll do it on my own." Eve fell in the trap and obeyed her flesh, and it cost her. It cost Adam. It cost all of humanity.

Rhonda and I often tell a little story from the early years of our marriage that's funny to us now. At the time we were newly married and having a little spat, when Rhonda said to me, "Adam, be careful what you let in the garden."

I had let some strife into the home. We don't normally do that, but we were just learning a lot of things. After she said that, I looked at her and responded, "Well, Eve, if I let a snake get by me, just don't talk to it." Actually, our instructions to "Adam" and "Eve" were good advice for us all. Men, don't let snakes in the garden. And, women, if a snake slips by, don't talk to it.

You see, God told Adam and Eve that they had authority and dominion over the garden and everything on the earth. God told Adam to till the garden and watch over it, guard it and protect it. So the first problem wasn't that Eve ate the fruit. The first problem was that Adam let down his guard; otherwise the snake would not have gotten in the garden. Adam wasn't being diligent or maybe he thought one snake was no problem, but he was wrong. It was a big problem!

"But I'm created in the likeness and image of God and these three categories of sin will never happen to me," someone might say.

Ouch—that very statement is prideful. I'm telling you that that kind of arrogance will get you in big trouble. We cannot afford to think that what happened to Eve could never happen to us.

It's one thing to be sure of who you are in Christ, but it's another thing altogether to think that you cannot be tempted or snared by sin. The minute you think that way, you're opening the door to trouble because God has already warned us through His Word that the devil will come at us through the lust of our eyes, the lust of our flesh and the pride of life. At some point or another, we all will be faced with "I want it. I want it. I want it."

Of course God wants us blessed. He wants us to have things, and He wants to meet the desires of our heart, but it's another thing altogether to lust after things. If we seek the kingdom of God first, everything else that will be a blessing to our lives will be added to us.

JESUS BEATS TEMPTATION

Over the years as a pastor, I've watched people begin to walk in the blessings of God, but not be able to continue in the walk because they didn't have enough Word in their hearts; the lusts of the flesh began to take over. Just as we have read in the parable of the sower (Mark 4), the Word gets choked out. Then the person no longer serves God. So these three categories of temptation are a serious thing, and we need to avoid them like the plague they are.

When you think about it, Eve showed us exactly how to fail when temptation comes our way; she was tempted and she sinned. On the other hand, Jesus was tempted and *did not* sin. Where Eve fell, Jesus won. That tells me that we can learn from Eve's mistakes, but we need to make Jesus our example of how to handle temptation. We need to follow His lead and take a closer look at how He handled temptation and won.

Actually, we've already outlined some of the devil's playbook when it comes to enticing us to sin. But the good news is that God has given us His playbook also. The devil obviously has strategies and patterns to get us off track, but God has turned us on to what they are and given us His strategies to win.

In Luke 4:2-24 we see the set of temptations that the devil used on Jesus. Luke 4 says that after Jesus returned from Jordan, the Spirit led Him into the wilderness where He was tempted by the devil for 40 days. The first thing the devil did was to tempt Jesus with the lust of his flesh. Jesus was tired and hungry, so the devil started by saying, "…If thou be the Son of God, command this stone that it be made bread" (verse 3).

"Is it even possible to turn stones to bread?" someone might ask. I'm pretty sure that Jesus could have done it; otherwise, it would not have been a legitimate temptation. After all, later in the Gospels Jesus turned water into wine.

Right from the start, during what we call the temptation of Christ, the devil immediately pulled out his temptation playbook and hit Jesus with some of his best moves. The first play he called out was the lust of the flesh. The devil figured since Jesus was hungry that he should start talking about food; he wanted Jesus thinking about loaves of bread.

How did Jesus refuse the temptation? Jesus looked the devil square in the face and boldly said, "It is written, That man shall not live by bread alone, but by every Word of God" (verse 4). How did Jesus defeat the devil? With the Word. That's one answer that we better put in our Overcoming Temptation Playbook. Jesus refused temptation by speaking the Word of God and using the exact scripture that pertained to the situation. What do you think that says about how you should handle temptation?

The next page from the devil's temptation playbook was taking Jesus to a high mountain and showing him all the kingdoms of the world.

The devil told Jesus that he would give them all back if Jesus would bow down and worship him. Actually, have you noticed that the devil often dangles in front of people what seems to be the end result of their goals?

The devil was offering Jesus a short cut to one of the very things Jesus came to do on this earth, which was to take back the authority Adam surrendered to the devil. While easier on Jesus' flesh to bypass the nasty crucifixion, the end result would have been the continued bondage of mankind to Satan and sin. The easy way out is seldom the right way.

How did Jesus handle this temptation? He told the devil no way. "Jesus answered and said unto him, Get thee behind me, Satan: for it is written, Thou shalt worship the Lord thy God, and him only shalt thou serve" (Luke 4:8). Jesus told the devil that Jesus worshiping the devil wasn't going to happen. Again, Jesus defeated the devil with the Word.

Finally, the devil brought Jesus to Jerusalem and set Him on the pinnacle of the temple to challenge Jesus about who He is. The devil's goal in this instance was to trick Jesus into questioning who He was. Remember, the devil sold Eve on the lie that God was trying to keep Adam and Eve from being gods. But Jesus knew the Word too well. Jesus knew who He was, and He knew He did not need to prove Himself to the devil.

The devil said to Jesus, "If you're really the son of God, then throw yourself down. The angels will protect you." Can you imagine the devil throwing scripture back at Jesus like that? As shocking as it is, we shouldn't be surprised; he does the same thing to you and me. The devil knows the Word of God well enough to pop up with scriptures. In fact, he can quote it and twist it and misconstrue it with the best of them, so keep that in mind the next time he starts talking to you.

But Jesus put the father of lies in his place and answered right back, saying, "...It is said, Thou shalt not tempt the Lord thy God" (verse 12). The devil had no choice but to leave Jesus alone and go find someone who didn't know the Word so well. Jesus correctly quoted scripture and correctly applied scripture. Bottom line: Scripture will get you out of temptation every time.

In Luke 4:14 it says, "Jesus returned in the power of the Spirit into Galilee: and there went out a fame of him through all the region round about." Refuse to give into temptations, and you will become stronger every time you withstand the enemy.

DRAWN AWAY BY LUST

We must understand that as born-again Christians, our citizenship is in heaven, and we should act like it. Even though we live on this earth, we should be foreigners and aliens down here and live a whole different lifestyle. First Peter 2:11 says, "Dearly beloved, I beseech you as *strangers and pilgrims*, abstain from fleshly lusts, which war against the soul."

As visitors on this planet, God expects us to refrain from carnal lusts that draw us into a strategic warfare the devil has designed for us. Eve obeyed her flesh, and it cost her. It cost Adam. It cost all of humanity. The devil would like nothing better than for all humanity—especially those who are born of God—to obey the impulses of the flesh. But God's Word and God's Spirit arm us with supernatural equipment to overcome.

CHAPTER 3
MY FLESH! MY FLESH!

Years ago I joked that someone should really take the time to make a list of sins, so there would be a universal awareness of exactly what sin is. But it wasn't long before I learned that the Bible already has such a list in Galatians 5.

"But why in the world would I want to read about a bunch of sins when I'm trying to stop sinning?" someone might ask. The answer is that we must thoroughly understand the problem—what sin is and how we get into sin—so we can get out of it and stay out of it. To win over sin, we need to take off the blinders, turn on the lights and look sin square in the face.

TURNING ON THE LIGHTS

Filled with compassion for some folks I was counseling, I asked the Lord in prayer one day why some folks struggle to get victory over sin even though Jesus already set them free. I asked Him why some people go around and around the same mountain, getting stuck in habits or bad behaviors and patterns in their lives.

This is what He spoke to my heart: Anytime a person repeatedly and consistently has the same issues—whether it be sin, insecurity, sickness or whatever—the person sits in darkness in that area.

Even if you're born again, Spirit filled and walk in the light of God's Word in many areas, if you struggle with sin on a consistent basis or you cannot seem to break free of sin's control in a particular area, in that area you sit in darkness. So, then, what gets rid of darkness?

Light.

Once you shine the light of God's Word on your situation, you're on your way out of the prison house; shackles cannot help but fall off.

When it comes to turning on the lights, 2 Corinthians 4:4 says the devil is the god of this world who blinds the eyes of the unbeliever lest he should see and be saved. So the No. 1 way to turn on the lights is to receive Jesus as Lord and Savior. Colossians 1:13 says at the moment a person receives Jesus he or she is translated out of the kingdom of darkness into the kingdom of light.

"Yeah, but since I'm a Christian, and I've been translated into the kingdom of light, how could I ever be in the dark again about anything?" someone might ask. The answer is that some Christians don't have revelation of God's Word in some particular areas of their lives. And where they don't have the Word, they don't have the light.

In the same way, John 8:32 says, "And you will know the Truth, and the Truth will set you free" (AMP). Likewise, if you don't know the truth, how can it set you free? It cannot. That's how the devil keeps people blinded.

The good news is that Jesus knows exactly how to turn the lights on for believers and unbelievers alike. Matthew 4:16 says, "The people which sat in darkness saw great light; and to them which sat in the region and shadow of death light is sprung up."

Habits, addictions and behavior patterns of sin have a nasty way of making people feel like helpless victims. I've dealt with people in these situations who've said it's a constant struggle and it makes their lives not worth living. But life is worth living because Jesus didn't just bring us the light; *He is the light.*

Whether the darkness of sin is a trap of the enemy that started when a person was young or it showed up yesterday, it makes no difference. God said He will deliver you out of your troubles. God wants you to have exceedingly, abundantly above all you could ever ask or think in this life (Ephesians 3:20). He wants you to live a life that's full and complete. Trouble will come along as long as you live on this earth, but God wants you to be victorious with nothing binding you.

You don't have to sit in darkness anymore. Isaiah 42:6 says, "I, the Lord, have called You in righteousness, And will hold Your hand; I will keep You and give You as a covenant to the people, As a light to the Gentiles" (NKJV). What does verse 7 say? "To open blind eyes, To bring out prisoners from the prison, Those who sit in darkness from the prison house" (NKJV).

Ephesians 1:18 says, "By having the eyes of your heart flooded with light, so that you can know and understand the hope to which He has called you, and how rich is His glorious inheritance in the saints (His set-apart ones)" (AMP). Psalm 119:130 says, "The entrance of Your words gives light; It gives understanding to the simple" (NKJV). That's what we're doing right now; we're turning the lights on.

If there's a habit or a pattern or something you need to change, then get real with God and say, "All right, Lord, You set me free some 2,000 years ago, so I'm done hanging around the prison house. I no longer want to be shackled to sin." Most people want out, but don't know how to get out. It starts right here. Say aloud: "Lord, take the blinders off my eyes and flood me with light. Shine Your light on me!"

I cannot promise you that the devil will never bother you again, not even on the longest day you live. But I can promise you that God has all the answers, and if you stick with Him, He will deliver you out of trouble. Jesus already paid the price for your freedom on the cross, and now He's trying to help you walk in it. Put on your sunglasses and keep reading. He's about to flood you with light.

DEFEATING SIN

We've seen that by shining the light of God's Word on sin, the way out of sin comes into focus. So let's shine a spotlight on temptations and enticements that come to us all. As we read about the lusts of the flesh highlighted in Galatians 5, the light will shine even brighter.

By looking at these sins one at a time, the Bible shows us how we can defeat these sins one at a time.

Most people are surprised to see what each category includes and how we can fall blindly into sin traps. In fact, a person might hear about the lusts of the flesh in Galatians and think, *These don't have anything to do with me. I don't have problem with things like witchcraft, emulations or seditions. I'm good. I don't do any of those.* Really? Are you so sure? Keep reading because these definitions hit us all right where we live. The truth is, every one of us can take an inventory sheet and find ourselves in one of these works of the flesh at one time or another.

Let's look at definitions for each work of the flesh listed.

> **Galatians 5:19-21**
> 19 Now the works of the flesh are manifest, which are these; Adultery, fornication, uncleanness, lasciviousness,
>
> 20 Idolatry, witchcraft, hatred, variance, emulations, wrath, strife, seditions, heresies,
>
> 21 Envyings, murders, drunkenness, revellings, and such like: of the which I tell you before, as I have also told you in time past, that they which do such things shall not inherit the kingdom of God.

ADULTERY

The word *adultery* in the Greek is *porneia*, which according to Strong's Exhaustive Concordance of the Bible means *to act the harlot*. It may go without saying, but it is where we get the word for pornography. Most of us realize that this sin occurs when there is sex and/or an inappropriate relationship outside marriage. But as we mentioned earlier, the act of adultery doesn't just happen out of the blue one day on the way home from the grocery store with no warning. No, *adultery first begins as a thought that eventually becomes an action*. No matter what it may seem like to a person, adultery simmers underneath the surface until it boils over the top. Attitudes and thoughts pop up that grow bigger and bigger until they're conceived into action.

In other words, the devil starts planting the thought of adultery by telling you that your spouse doesn't appreciate you. He points out all the ways you are dissatisfied at home and all the things you're missing at home. He lies and tells you that marriage doesn't need to be a lifetime proposition with one person. Then the devil sees to it that just the right person comes across your path to provide maximum temptation. The devil knows exactly how to sell it, too.

So how do we resist this particular work of the flesh? First and foremost let's look at 1 Thessalonians 5:22, which says, "Abstain from all appearance of evil." That may sound simple, but it's profound. And it's really good advice. If you want to stay far from adultery, then don't put yourself in a compromising situation. Here's the bottom line: If a situation looks wrong, it is wrong.

Maybe a situation doesn't look wrong to the world, but does it look wrong to your Master and Lord? Does it seem wrong in your spirit? If so, that's the Holy Spirit giving you an uneasy feeling in your spirit. If you back away when you get those uneasy feelings, you can save yourself a world of heartache and trouble.

Romans 6:13 says, "Neither yield ye your members as instruments of unrighteousness unto sin: but yield yourselves unto God, as those that are alive from the dead, and your members as instruments of righteousness unto God." You might wonder, *What does it look like when you yield your members as instruments of unrighteousness?* It's being at the wrong place with the wrong people at the wrong time. It's looking and wondering and fantasizing about the wrong people, and it's sharing intimately with the wrong people.

That is exactly what yielding your members to unrighteousness looks like even before the act of adultery, and if you remain on that course, you'll likely land in adultery. God tells us to yield our members to righteousness, which means that everything we do in relationships—even the small things—should be proper and pleasing to Him.

FORNICATION

The next work of the flesh is fornication, which is a sexual relationship outside of marriage. The root word in the Greek is the same word *porneia* used for adultery. Therefore, adultery and fornication are actually the same word in the Greek, though the King James translators separated the two words for clarity.

I know the world sneers and laughs, but God's Word plainly teaches that sex should be reserved only for marriage. The Bible says that when a man and a woman unite in intercourse, they become one. It's an important act designed to create a permanent bond, linking man and woman spirit, soul and body.

No wonder so many people in our society are confused. Many people freely share themselves in a way that God reserved for marriage, but then wonder how and why they end up in such big messes in life.

Nevertheless, fornication doesn't happen out of the blue any more than adultery does. Sin is a process, and just like with adultery, fornication begins with thoughts that eventually become actions.

UNCLEANNESS

The word *uncleanness* in the Greek is *akatharsia*, which according to Strong's Exhaustive Concordance of the Bible, means *impurity (the quality) physically or morally*. The Life Applicatioin New Testament Commentary defines *uncleanness* as moral uncleaness. The reference says, "Perhaps no sexual act has taken place, but the person exhibits a crudeness or insensitivity in sexual matters that offends others." Uncleanness amounts to vulgar or unclean thoughts the devil brings to our minds. Most people don't understand that every thought they think is not their own. The devil is very efficient at bringing all kinds of thoughts—lewd and unclean imaginings, doubt, fear, panic and the list goes on.

You name it, if it leads to destruction or temptation, the devil will drag it before your mind. The devil is after control of your thought life because unclean and vulgar thoughts eventually produce unclean and vulgar actions. Therefore, to control your actions, you must control your mind.

Maybe you've noticed that the devil also tries to bring up imaginations and memories from your life of sin before you were born again. It's like he walks around with a photo album to embarrass and harass you. But when a thought or a mental picture or imagination comes before you that is lewd or unclean or just plain unwanted, do as 2 Corinthians 10:4-5 says and cast it down. How? Open your mouth and boldly say, "I refuse that thought in Jesus' name! I am a new creature in Christ Jesus!" You can take harassing thoughts captive every time by speaking God's Word, which we'll talk more about in Chapter 8.

Unfortunately, some people don't do anything when these rogue thoughts begin firing at their minds, and it gets them into trouble. Don't ignore bad thoughts or deny them; arrest them and replace them. Stop wrong thoughts before they become wrong actions. Controlling your thought life is vital to walking with God and overcoming sin.

LASCIVIOUSNESS

The next work of the flesh is *lasciviousness* or extreme overeating or wild, out-of-control living. It comes from the Greek word *aselgeia*. According to Vine's Expository Dictionary, it "denotes excess, licentiousness, absence of restraint, indeceny, wantonness." The Life Application New Testament Commentary says, "The person has no sesne of shame or restraint." In other words, the flesh does not like to be disciplined at all. Period. Yet, to let our flesh eat excessively or live a wild life is not godly living, and it will open up our lives to sin. I didn't say this; God's Word does.

You might say, "Well, I've tried and tried to get certain behaviors under control, but it hasn't worked." The good news is that you don't have to do this on your own. You have God and His Word to help you.

First Corinthians 9:25 says, "...every man that striveth for the mastery is temperate in all things...." The words *temperate in all things* are key words that speak of bringing the body in line. How do we do it? On purpose. We must diligently pursue a lifestyle of moderation whether we're talking about food or any other thing. Bottom line, we should not be excessive in any area.

We also need to do what Romans 13:14 teaches, "Put on the Lord Jesus Christ, and make no provision for the flesh, to fulfill its lusts" (NKJV). When we clothe ourselves with Jesus, there will be no room for lasciviousness.

IDOLATRY

The next work of the flesh you should avoid is idolatry. You might think, I do not have any idols sitting around my house, so let's move on to the next one. Not so fast. The word *idolatry* comes from the Greek word *eidoloatres*, and according to The Life Application New Testament Commentary, it refers to a person who "creates substitutes for God and then treats them as if they were God." The act of idolatry is not just bowing down to a statue. It could be anything or anyone who comes between us and our relationship with God. It would also mean any excessive attachment or veneration for anything or anyone; when we adore something or someone more than God, then idolatry is a problem. This definition could single out so many things in our lives that hit most folk right where they live.

Frankly, as a pastor for more than 19 years, I've seen believers elevate people, careers, houses, sports, hobbies, possessions and many other things above God. Most people don't admit with their words that they elevate things above God, but they prove it by their actions.

Thank God for the Bible that tells us how to stay free from idolatry. First Corinthians 10:14 in The Amplified Bible says, "Therefore, my dearly beloved, shun (keep clear away from, avoid by flight if need be) any sort of idolatry (of loving or venerating anything more than God)." Do you love and honor anything or anyone more than God? Maybe you've been living in idolatry and don't even know it. If so, you can resist with God's Word and His compassionate nature.

There's nothing wrong with putting your all into a career and working hard to succeed, but if your career comes before your relationship with the Lord, then you are in trouble. The Lord is not against your success—quite the opposite. God is all for success, but He's all for it in the correct order. God must be No. 1 in your life.

WITCHCRAFT

The next work of the flesh is witchcraft, and the interesting thing is, most Christians are sure this sin does not apply to them. But wait until you understand what this word really means.

The Greek word translated *witchcraft* is actually *pharmakeia*, which is the root word from which we get *pharmacy*. Vine's Expository Dictionary says witchcraft is the use of medicine, drugs, spells, poisoning and even sorcery. In other words, witchcraft describes how the flesh attempts to medicate itself to escape from things. In our society, many people medicate their flesh by abusing legal and illegal drugs or alcohol; many people medicate with food.

Why is this work of the flesh so prevalent in the world today? I believe it's because people are hurting, and they don't like their lives. I'm so glad God has a better answer found in Luke 4.

> **Luke 4:18 (NKJV)**
> **18 The Spirit of the Lord is upon Me,**
> **Because He has anointed Me To preach the**
> **gospel to the poor; He has sent Me to heal**
> **the brokenhearted, To proclaim liberty to the**
> **captives and recovery of sight to the blind,**
> **To set at liberty those who are oppressed.**

Broken hearts are not uncommon because life can deliver some pretty hard knocks, but Jesus came to heal the brokenhearted. If we will let Jesus heal our hurts, we will not need to medicate. The Lord wants us to turn to Him instead of turning to substances temporarily or long term. There's no reason to turn over our flesh to abuses when we have a Savior able to heal every hurt.

HATRED

Another work of the flesh is hatred, which comes from the Greek word *echthra*. According to Vine's Expository Dictionary, it means exactly what we think it means: to hate. It is used especially to describe "malicious and unjustifiable feelings toward others, whether toward the innocent or by mutual animosity." People who yield to hatred hold grudges and harbor deep resentments with roots of bitterness. How do we get rid of this work of hatred? The Bible once again gives us the answer.

> **1 John 2:5-6 (NKJV)**
> 5 But whoever keeps His word, truly the love of God is perfected in him. By this we know that we are in him.
> 6 He who says he abides in Him ought himself also to walk just as He walked.

We must combat hatred with the Word of God. First, we must obey God's Word. Second, we must let the love of God be perfected or matured in us. Third, we must learn to abide in Him and live vitally united with Him, so His ways, His thoughts and His Word become ours. Fourth, we must walk on this earth as He walked. Jesus never hated anyone, and we must imitate Him.

These works of the flesh have everything to do with you and me. They affect our everyday lives. Maybe there's one you or I battle more or less than the others, but we all have the opportunity to deal with them continually in life.

VARIANCE

Another work of the flesh is variance, which comes from the Greek word *eris*. According to Strong's Exhaustive Concordance of the Bible, it is "of uncertain affinity; quarrel, i.e. (by implication) wrangling." The Life Application New Testament Commentary says it like this: "Quarreling—competition, rivalry, bitter conflict—the seeds and the natural fruit of hatred." The person involved in variance is a person who is quarrelsome. The person is contentious and likes to cause controversy.

This person is the type who feels he or she always has to be right. I think this starts when a person believes that being wrong is a weakness, which is an opinion our society enhances. Consequently, the person who gives in to variance exaggerates or makes excuses or even lies to protect his or her position.

How do we escape this work of the flesh? We must read, study and absorb God's Word. We'll look at scriptures on this topic more specifically in chapters to come, but basically we must reprogram our minds to think like God thinks. Our old nature may have given way to variance, but our new born-again nature should refuse variance and its chaotic way. We don't need to be right all the time; in fact, it's good for us to admit when we're wrong.

If we will purpose to renew our minds every day, variance won't be able to lodge itself in our thinking. I guarantee that getting rid of variance in our lives will make a big difference in our marriages, our families and our friendships.

You might be thinking, *It's so much work to get out of sin; how can I really stay free?* The truth is, you need help. And you have all the help you need—the Holy Spirit. He's your helper, and He's on call 24/7 to help you get out of sin and stay out sin.

EMULATIONS

The word *emulations* is from the Greek word *zelos*. Vine's Expository Dictionary defines it as *to be jealous, to burn with jealousy*. This person is not only jealous, but also moves with malice to get what he or she envies.

This person desires to be superior to others and tries to create rivalries, and consequently, the person often puts other people down to get what he or she wants. While this description might be true before a person is born again, it should not be true after.

Maybe you have heard a person say, "I've got a bad temper because I have red hair." Or "I'm Irish, and we get worked up easily." Bless their hearts, the red-haired people of the world and the Irish have taken a bad rap. You and I must put all that kind of talk down because it's carnal, and we have the power of the Holy Spirit living inside us.

It doesn't make any difference what your hair color is or what your ethnic background is, you can rule over your flesh. Don't ever buy into the lie that you cannot help yourself because God said you can.

The Spirit of God dealt with me recently that the way to overcome the flesh is to get so full of God that carnal things get pushed out. We don't need to focus on what's wrong; we need to focus on God's Word that fixes what's wrong. God's Word will drive out what's wrong. Sure, we'll still have to pass up sin and keep our bodies under control, but it's a whole lot easier when we're wall-to-wall God on the inside.

We've probably all displayed emulations in our lives, but our mission is to overcome this nasty work of the flesh. The love of God is how it's done. You might think, *I wish I had that God kind of love.* If you're born again, you do. Romans 5:5 says "...the love of God has been poured out in our hearts by the Holy Spirit who was given to us" (NKJV).

Whether you feel like it or not has nothing to do with it. If you're born again, it's in there; God said He put it in there. What you must realize is that we're not talking about a feeling; we're talking about a choice. You must *choose* to walk in love, and when you do, the love of God will shut down emulations. After all, God wants us to rejoice with others not compete with them. Jealousy, agitation and irritation are ugly; we need to put God's love to work in our lives instead.

The Word tells us how to do that in 1 Corinthians.

> **1 Corinthians 13:4-8 (AMP)**
> 4 Love endures long and is patient and kind; love never is envious nor boils over with jealousy, is not boastful or vainglorious, does not display itself haughtily.
>
> 5 It is not conceited (arrogant and inflated with pride); it is not rude (unmannerly) and does not act unbecomingly. Love (God's love in us) does not insist on its own rights or its own way, for it is not self-seeking; it is not touchy or fretful or resentful; it takes no account of the evil done to it [it pays no attention to a suffered wrong].
>
> 6 It does not rejoice at injustice and unrighteousness, but rejoices when right and truth prevail.
>
> 7 Love bears up under anything and everything that comes, is ever ready to believe the best of every person, its hopes are fadeless under all circumstances, and it endures everything [without weakening].
>
> 8 Love never fails [never fades out or becomes obsolete or comes to an end]. . . .

When we walk in this God kind of love, we will not give into emulations or any other work of the flesh. When we walk in God's love, we will never fail.

How much more could possibly be wrong with my flesh? you might wonder. The truth is, before we were born again, there wasn't anything right with our flesh. Our flesh inherited its makeup from this fallen world's system, and that's why our flesh has trouble living sin free. But thank God for His Word that helps us live a life pleasing to the Lord. Every born-again person wants to please God; it's in our new DNA. In the next several chapters, we'll see how God gives us many supernatural tools, weapons and helps to live a sin-free life.

WRATH

The Bible describes the next work of the flesh as wrath, which is really no mystery at all. The word *wrath* comes from the original Greek word *thumos*, describing a person in constant anger. The Life Application New Testament Commentary offers this definition of wrath: "Outburst of anger—selfish anger. The plural form conveys the meaning of continual and uncontrolled behavior."

We've all encountered a wrathful person who could blow up at any minute in any situation. Frankly, no one wants to be around this volatile walking, talking human explosive capable of causing widespread destruction. No one likes to go out with a person like this because it's impossible to know what the wrathful person will say or do at a restaurant, a sporting event or a store or when the person will embarrass everyone with another display of anger. Wrathful folks are explosions ready to blow and disasters waiting to happen.

So what should you do if you just happen to be one of these hotheads? How can you change your *thumos* to a stable demeanor? How can you go from explosive to smooth and calm? The Bible has the answers. In fact, the chapters that follow will outline many helps for every work of the flesh, but let's focus here on a picture James gives us of a cool, calm, collected Christian.

> **James 1:19-20 (NKJV)**
> 19 So then, my beloved brethren, let every man be swift to hear, slow to speak, slow to wrath;
>
> 20 for the wrath of man does not produce the righteousness of God.

These instructions may sound simple, but they really get the job done. Notice again the three keys these scriptures give us:

(1) Be a good listener

(2) Don't rush to talk

(3) Don't get mad quickly

It makes a lot of sense to be a good listener and really understand what people are saying. In fact, have you ever been in a heated discussion with people who didn't hear a word you were saying because they were too busy "loading their guns"? Instead of trying to understand what you were saying, they were collecting bullets to fire at you during the next round.

We all know that feeling when a person isn't listening; he or she is just getting ready to blast us and blow us out of the water. It might be funny to think about, but it's not right. It's fleshly, and as Christians, we cannot allow ourselves to behave that way.

The next point is to be slow to speak, which is a real challenge for some people. But have you ever noticed that just because you *can* say something, doesn't mean you *should* say something? I've heard people say, "Well, I'm the kind of person who has to speak my mind." "I've got to get this off my chest!" "I'm going to give that person a piece of my mind!" No, please don't.

If your mind is not renewed with the Word of God, then the first thought that comes to your mind is probably not a godly thought. So let me suggest that you hold on to it. I think we'd all be better off if most people would filter their thoughts before they pop out of their mouths.

Let me throw in a little marriage counseling by saying that if more people would put their hands over their mouths—and use their ears instead—we'd have happier couples. Folks, our ears are not hooks on the side of our heads to hang earrings; they are to improve hearing and show each other that we can hear.

The right words can bring peace to a situation and disarm anger; the wrong words inflame it. Maybe somewhere in the world there are a few pious married couples who have only had one argument in 20 or more years of marriage. The rest of the married folks I know have learned that speaking the wrong words in anger is like throwing gasoline on a fire. Instant combustion is the result.

Doing things God's way can save all the charred remains. The Bible says simply to be swift to hear, slow to speak and slow to get mad.

James also points out the importance of being a doer of the Word in verse 22, which says "…be doers of the word, and not hearers only, deceiving yourselves." You see, it's not enough to go to church on Sunday. If you want to live sin free, you must put God's Word to practice in your life all seven days of the week. If you don't, the Bible itself says you will be deceived.

When people are deceived about the works of their flesh, they think they cannot help but sin. That's a lie! We can control our flesh. We can subdue it. We can crucify it. We can change. And God will help us.

James explains yet another very important component of combating wrath in verse 26, which says, "If anyone among you thinks he is religious, and does not bridle his tongue but deceives his own heart, this one's religion *is* useless" (NKJV). Does this verse mean that we're supposed to buy some expensive contraption to lock down our tongue? No, it's as simple as the instructions from my Mamaw, "Just keep your mouth shut." She used to say, like many of us have heard, "If you don't have anything good to say, don't say anything at all." Keeping your mouth shut can be a godly and spiritual thing to do.

I'm not telling you to be a doormat. I'm not telling you to keep quiet when someone wrongs you or cheats you. I'm not telling you that you cannot be straightforward and speak up. What I am telling you is this: No wrath allowed.

STRIFE

The next work of the flesh is strife, a huge issue for many. Actually, there are few Christians who don't have the opportunity to deal with strife on a regular basis. It's a constant and dangerous enemy, but with God's help we can defeat it.

The word *strife* in the original Greek is *erithia,* and according to Strong's Exhaustive Concordance of the Bible, it is either translated contention or strife. The real issue with strife is that it means a person's principal concern is getting whatever he or she wants at any cost. People who operate in this work of the flesh will say anything and sacrifice anyone or anything to achieve their desired end while blind to injuring others along the way.

The Bible has something very ominous to say about strife in James 3:16, which says, "Where envying and strife is, there is confusion and every evil work." One thing I've learned about God is that He doesn't exaggerate. So when God says where strife exists there is every evil work, He means it. Strife is an open invitation for the devil to play around in your life and wreak havoc.

This is no exaggeration. Don't mess with any of these works of the flesh, but especially be on guard for this one. Crucify fleshly lusts that lead you into strife because the price tag is way too high.

As a pastor I take extra precaution when it comes to strife in our church. I tell every new member that Rhonda and I will love them through anything—backsliding, sin, divorce or whatever. But if people cause strife in our church, I will ask them to leave. Since strife opens the door to every evil work, it's no wonder why many churches don't have the power of God like they should. Let me encourage you to determine there will be no strife for you—not in your family, not in your work place, not in your church and not anywhere in your life.

Trust me. The devil will throw opportunities to get into strife at you left and right because the Bible says he comes immediately for the Word's sake. You'll probably have an opportunity to resist strife soon since you've been reading scriptures on avoiding strife. It's inevitable since the devil comes immediately for the Word's sake (Mark 4:17).

I remember when Rhonda and I first got married, it seemed like every Wednesday we found ourselves arguing. Yet, it didn't take us long to figure out that the devil was trying to get us out of unity so we could not minister at the Wednesday night church service.

The devil has tricks he pulls on you, too. Maybe you have little Johnny fussing in the back of the car on the way to church. You want to go to one restaurant, but little Johnny wants McDonalds and he throws a fit. It's hard to hold on to your joy, but hold on anyway. The devil is working hard to get you into strife because he wants to bring every evil work your way. For one thing, strife will bring your faith to a screeching halt. Your profession of faith won't override strife. Frankly, you can confess and pray all you want—until you're blue in the face—but if you're in strife, your faith won't work for you.

Confession isn't going to work for Billy Bob if he's at home screaming at his wife morning, noon and night. You probably know a Billy Bob and everywhere he goes, strife goes. He causes strife at work. He causes strife at church. And he definitely causes strife at home.

So how should Billy Bob steer clear of strife and how should we? Galatians 5:25 says, "If we live in the Spirit, let us also walk in the Spirit." We'll talk more about walking in the spirit in Chapter 6. Meanwhile, let's choose to avoid strife at every turn and save ourselves a whole lot of trouble.

SEDITIONS

Another work of the flesh is seditions, which sounds ominous. Actually, I think because we have believed these works of the flesh sounded so ominous, we were sure they didn't apply to us. Unfortunately, we're finding they all do.

This word is from the Greek word *dichostsis*, which according to Strong's Exhaustive Concordance of the Bible, means *dissention*. The person involved in sedition is one who causes division, dissention and insurrections. In simpler terms the person loves drama. This work of the flesh stirs up commotion and keeps things in an uproar.

It's interesting that the word *insurrection* is included in this definition because an insurrection happens when someone revolts against the established authority. Think about it. When you and I rebel against authority, it's also a form of sedition. The word *sedition* makes rebellion sound a whole lot more serious, doesn't it? The truth is, it is serious. In all my years of ministry, I've watched this work of the flesh operate many times in many people. I've learned that if sedition isn't eradicated the minute it surfaces, it will blow up and really hurt people. Of course, the devil loves it when we yield to our flesh; that's his playground.

A person yielding to sedition defies those in authority over them such as pastors, leaders, parents, bosses or whomever. Doesn't that sound like a trademark of the devil who defied God's authority and got kicked out of heaven? Let's make sure we don't go the same route and defy God's authority. Let's also determine never to let the enemy use us to defy those who have been placed over us in authority. We should have a reputation for being loyal.

HERESIES

The definition of *heresies* totally surprised me. I thought heresies were wrong doctrines, but actually it has more to do with how we think about ourselves. We get the word *heresies* from the Greek word *hairesis*, which according to The Life Application New Testament Commentary, is defined as, "the feeling that everyone is wrong except those in your own little group—dissension created among people because of divisions. Thus describes the tendency to look for allies in conflict. The almost spontaneous generation of cliques demonstrates this characteristic of sinful human desires."

Bottom line, heresies amount to us thinking that we are better than others. It's like high school all over again—back to a clique mentality. But when you think about it, the clique mentality was bad enough in high school; we don't need this mentality in the body of Christ or the local church.

On one hand, it's human nature for birds of feather to flock together, but on the other hand, hanging with the wrong people who are of like mentality can get us into trouble. The Bible plainly tells us in 1 Corinthians 15:33, "Bad company corrupts good morals" (NASB). James also tells us to beware of treating people differently when he says, "If you show servile regard (prejudice, favoritism) for people, you commit sin and are rebuked and convicted by the Law as violators and offenders" (James 2:9 AMP).

We are to love our neighbors as ourselves according to the royal law, so it's wrong to judge our neighbors by how they look, dress, talk or any other external factor. The Bible tells us to treat other people like we want to be treated without partiality. If we do, we will not adhere to heresy.

ENVYINGS

The next work of the flesh listed in Galatians is *envyings*, which comes from the Greek word *phthonos*. According to Vine's Expository Dictionary, "envy is the feeling of displeasure produced by witnessing or hearing of the advantage or prosperity of others." Envy is when a person so deeply resents another's blessing that he or she attempts to take another person's blessing.

Maybe someone pulls up in a brand new bright red sports car and you fold your arms thinking, *Well now, look at that. Isn't that special. I'm a tither. Where's mine?* That's envy. And that's an attitude that needs adjusting; the Bible says to rejoice with those who rejoice.

Maybe you need to bless those who have been blessed. Maybe the best way to bring your attitude in line is to give the new car owner money to help make his or her payment. Maybe to pull your attitude in line you need to wash or detail the person's new car because sometimes it's necessary to get radical to put the flesh under. "I'd never do that," someone might say, "If that guy has enough money to buy that car, he can pay to get his own car cleaned up." Now there's a case of envy running wild.

This same attitude is not immune from the workplace; these envious attitudes go to work with people every day. Maybe a co-worker has a position you don't think he or she deserves and you want it. Instead of being kind, gracious and supportive of the person, you struggle with envy. "Yeah, but, the person really didn't deserve the position. I should have gotten it."

Maybe so, but you're not supposed to be looking at the world's system to obtain blessings or promotions. "I think I'll just go tell the boss what I know about So and So." That won't do any good; it will probably do a lot of bad. More than anything, that tells me that you're trusting in man's way, not God's ways.

The Bible tells us more about envy in James 3:14, which says, "But if you have bitter jealousy (envy) and contention (rivalry, selfish ambition) in your hearts, do not pride yourselves on it and thus be in defiance of and false to the truth" (AMP). You can see that envy and jealousy bring us in defiance to the truth of God's Word. So how do we deal with envy?

James 4:2 says, "You are jealous and covet [what others have] and your desires go unfulfilled; [so] you become murderers. [To hate is to murder as far as your hearts are concerned.] You burn with envy and anger and are not able to obtain [the gratification, the contentment, and the happiness that you seek], so you fight and war. You do not have, because you do not ask" (AMP).

The answer to envy is to get in faith and ask God for whatever it is that you desire and receive the blessing for yourself. God is not a respecter of persons by need or desire, but He is a respecter of faith. As you and I learn to ask God in faith, we will never have to be envious or jealous again.

MURDERS

Murders is not in the original language so I am not including it here. However, the Bible does say, "Whoever hates his brother is a murderer, and you know that no murderer has eternal life abiding in him" (1 John 3:15).

DRUNKENESS

Drunkeness comes from the word *methe*, and in the Greek means *habitual intoxication*. Why start something that could potentially lead to your destruction? My advice is just to say no!

REVELLINGS

The last work of the flesh we will concentrate on is revellings, which comes from the Greek word *komoi*. According to Strong's Exhaustive Concordance of the Bible, revellings is defined as "a carousal (as if letting loose)." This is someone who always needs to be entertained. The person of revellings is someone who likes to party. This is someone who continually keeps occupied so the person doesn't have to face what is wrong in his or her life.

This reminds me of when I was backslidden and away from God years ago, and I couldn't be in a room without some noise. I had to have the television or the radio blaring; something had to be going on around me.

This kind of person is always moving and cannot sit still because there's a work of the flesh that needs to be brought under control. Usually these folks avoid quiet because they don't want to deal with a personal issue or hurt. Yet, the best way to deal with it is to let Jesus minister to the soul.

Too often people who cannot stand to be alone and sit quietly have an ache on the inside that can't be fixed by humanity, by a doctor or by anything at all. So these people keep so busy they don't have to deal with themselves. But Luke 4 says that Jesus came to heal the brokenhearted, and I'm telling you that Jesus can heal restlessness on the inside of you.

Jesus healed me. In 1986, when I was working as an accountant in Indianapolis, my sister, Robin, dragged me to church, and I came back to the Lord and got filled with the Holy Spirit. My life suddenly and dramatically changed. I got full of God, and He began to heal what was broken on the inside of me.

It was no time at all before I would catch myself reading my Bible in a room with no noise at all. Before that time, there's no way I would have sat still or sat quietly. I had to have something going all the time, and I couldn't stand silence. But God touched my life with overwhelming peace, and there's no price tag that can measure its value.

Maybe you know someone like this who is always moving, always going, always craving noise. Maybe there's something on the inside of that person that needs to be fixed, and I'm telling you that Jesus is the One to do the fixing.

Attention workaholics: Let God bless you and prosper you. But if you're spending 120 hours a week at your job or your business, you've got a problem that needs to be fixed. If you're someone who's always on the go and can't sit still, I guarantee there's something in your soul that needs to be fixed. It's one thing to be busy, but it's another thing altogether to drive yourself to extremes. God doesn't want you to allow your flesh to dominate you and drive you to sin or even drive you overboard doing good; God doesn't want your flesh driving you in any way.

Refuse to give into your flesh. Refuse to allow anything to come between you and God, which would also mean that nothing should come between you and church, you and Bible reading, and you and prayer.

We must allow the Holy Spirit to dominate our lives, and we must give the spiritual arena of our lives first place. When we do, our flesh will be put under, and we will walk in life and peace. The reason many people cannot sit still and enjoy peace and fellowship with God is because of a soulish problem that needs to be put under. Yet by concentrating on things of the spirit, we put our souls at peace.

As we've broken down the definitions of the works of the flesh, most of us probably expected obtuse and complicated explanations for each word. What we have found are definitions that hit most of us where we live. What we have found are issues we all deal with on a regular basis.

In fact, I can imagine people saying, "We already knew we sinned. We didn't need to know about even more sins." But we did! We've turned the lights on, and now we need to find the escape clause for people looking to get out of sin.

CHAPTER 4
AN ESCAPE THEOLOGY

People often ask if it's really possible to escape temptation and sin, and I enjoy telling them that it's absolutely possible—no doubt about it. In fact, let me share an entire escape theology found in the Bible. There's no question in my mind that God wants us to escape temptation every time it comes along and that's why He lays out an escape route for you and me.

The Bible has a lot to say about escaping temptation, so let's begin by considering 1 Corinthians 10:13, a scripture many folks often use and abuse or at least quote incorrectly. Maybe you've even heard people say, "God will never give you more than you can bear." But it's important that we quote the whole scripture and understand what the Lord really is telling us:

> 1 Corinthians 10:13 (NKJV)
> No temptation has overtaken you except such as is common to man; but God is faithful, who will not allow you to be

tempted beyond what you are able, but with the temptation will also make the way of escape, that you may be able to bear it.

Many people pull out of context the phrase that says, "God… will not suffer you to be tempted above what you are able." If people focus on that part of the verse alone, and don't study it thoroughly, they will come to the wrong conclusion. They might mistakenly believe that God is the One who hands out suffering, implying that He gives a person only as much suffering as he or she can bear.

Some people even take this scripture to mean that toward the end of a temptation or trial, God will eventually rescue them after they've taken all they can handle. Is that true? Is that Bible? Is that what you and I are to take away from this scripture? No. Let's read the verse in The Amplified Bible to amplify its meaning.

> **1 Corinthians 10:13 (AMP)**
> For no temptation (no trial regarded as enticing to sin), [no matter how it comes or where it leads] has overtaken you and laid hold on you that is not common to man [that is, no temptation or trial has come to you that is beyond human resistance and that is not adjusted and adapted and belonging to human experience, and such as man can bear]. But God is faithful [to His Word and to His compassionate nature], and He [can be trusted] not to let you be tempted and tried and assayed beyond your ability and strength of resistance and power to endure, but with the temptation He will [always] also provide the way out (the means of escape to a landing place), that you may be capable and strong and powerful to bear up under it patiently.

This scripture lays out exactly how we can live a sin-free life. First of all, it says that temptation is common to all of us. No one ever arrives at a place where he or she is no longer tempted. If you're looking for that place of no more temptation, you'll have to wait until you go to heaven. As long as you live in a body, and there's a devil on this earth, you will face temptation.

This scripture also makes it clear that temptation is not beyond human resistance. That means it doesn't matter what a temptation is, how it comes or when it comes, you can resist it. Did you get that?

*You **can** resist it!*

People have told me with tears in their eyes, "I cannot get over this sin. It's too hard. God must have made me this way. This must be my cross to bear." No. That's not right; that's not Bible. No sin has been given to you by God as your "cross to bear" because sin always leads to death, and God is never the author of death. God already sent Jesus to pay for the sins of all who would believe in Him.

It's a major lie of the devil to convince people that they cannot resist sin. Actually, the devil and religion tell people all the time to simply learn to live with sin. But God says you can resist it and walk free. No way do you or I have to just put up with sin in our lives.

The third insight this scripture offers is that God is faithful. God never lies, and He can be fully trusted with your life and your deliverance from sin. However, if you're going to receive anything from God, it must begin with you believing God's Word and believing God keeps His Word. You must put your trust in Him so He can bring His Word to pass in your life. In order to live a life free from sin, fear and failure, you must recognize that God is not part of your problem; He is your only answer. You can count on Him, and He will never disappoint you.

Notice again the last phrase of 1 Corinthians 10:13, which says, "…God is faithful [to His word and to His compassionate nature], and He [can be trusted] not to let you be tempted and tried and assayed beyond your ability and strength of resistance and power to endure…" (AMP). He's promising you faithfulness, and you have His Word on it.

The very next phrase contains the Bible's great escape clause that says, "...but with the temptation He will [always] also provide the way out (*the means of escape to a landing place*), that you may be capable and strong and powerful to bear up under it patiently" (AMP).

Think about that for a minute. God's Word is saying that *you* have the ability and the strength of resistance and the power to endure temptation and come out on top. The scripture is talking about *you*. If you're tempted by something—no matter what it is—the Bible says you can bear it, you can endure it. God Himself says you can deal with it, you can overcome it, you can rise above it.

You can win.

Unfortunately, many people automatically assume that 1 Corinthians 10:13 tells us that we're stuck with a certain temptation and we have to live and endure it forever and carry it around like a badge. No way.

Now let me ask: How does this scripture say you should bear up during temptation? God's Word says to be capable, strong and powerful to bear up under it *patiently*. Notice patience is required. You may not just deal with a certain temptation once or even twice. But if you keep applying God's Word, walking in the Spirit and resisting the devil, you will be able to win over sin.

Patience has become a foul word in our vocabulary; no one wants to be patient day in and day out. If it's not drive-thru service, we don't want anything to do with it. But let me be honest. Sometimes we must keep after things for a while in order to achieve victory. What choice do we have? It all comes down to this: We either learn to resist temptation and sin by walking in the spirit, or we yield to temptation and fall into sin, and ultimately take home a paycheck of death.

Resistance is not futile; it always works in the kingdom of God. Plan to escape every temptation that comes your way by patiently using God's Word as your escape route. When you do, you will always land in a safe place. Keep after the temptation no matter what it is and no matter how many times it comes. Determine that sin, and consequently, death is not an option for you.

You can resist.

You can escape.

You can go and sin no more.

THE GREAT ESCAPE

The Bible provides a clear road map of how to escape the temptation to sin. In fact, we find the answer in Hebrews 2:3, which says, "How shall we escape if we neglect so great salvation. ..." The truth is, we won't escape if we neglect our salvation. But we will escape if we attend to our salvation, so let's take a closer look at how to attend to our salvation.

The word *salvation* means being born again, but it also means much more. In fact, the word *salvation* found in the New Testament is a Greek word that means deliverance, safety, preservation, healing and soundness. In other words, *salvation* includes the sum total of all blessings that God bestowed on mankind through Jesus' redemption for us on the cross.

Obviously, then, we cannot neglect our salvation and be empowered to avoid sin because salvation establishes our relationship with God. To avoid sin, we must first and foremost receive Jesus Christ as our Lord and Savior. That's definitely the most important decision we can ever make, and it's just the beginning. Receiving Jesus Christ is the first step through the door to a whole new life. But your new Christian walk is just that—a walk—and there are many more steps to take in God.

Before we go further, if you're not born again, let me encourage you to turn to Page 165 now and commit your life to Jesus. It will be the first step to turning your back on sin and escaping the corruption sin brings. If you are already born again, then let me challenge you to dig in and understand the full extent of the freedom that's already been provided to you.

DIVINE NATURE

As we attend to our salvation, we can fully partake of the divine nature of God Himself. In fact, God has given us exceedingly great and precious promises that enable us to partake fully of His divine nature and escape the corruption in the world. Let's read more about these promises that have the power to free us from sin and death.

> **2 Peter 1:3-4 (NKJV)**
> 3 As His divine power has given to us all things that *pertain* to life and godliness, through the knowledge of Him who called us by glory and virtue,
>
> 4 by which have been given to us exceedingly great and precious promises, that through these you may be partakers of the divine nature, having escaped the corruption *that is* in the world through lust.

This scripture tells us that through the "exceedingly great and precious promises, we can be partakers of the divine nature." So what does it mean to *partake?* Well, on occasion, I like to partake of coconut cream pie. I see it. I seize it. I put it in my mouth, and I happily partake.

Yet, if I partake of too much coconut cream pie, it begins to show. As a matter of fact, we can tell what people partake of on a regular basis because it always shows. That's why God says if you will partake of My Word, My divine nature will show on you.

Can it get any better than that? Peter is telling us that if we will delve into God's Word that we will get full of God Himself. Peter is telling us that we can get so full of the divine nature of God that it will show on us; it will be obvious and evident for all to see.

Think about that for a minute. If you need more divine nature to show up on the outside of you, maybe you need to spend more time partaking of God's Word and God's Spirit. After all, what will this new nature do when it shows up on you? The last part of the verse says it will enable you and empower you to escape corruption through lust. What does the lust of our flesh produce? Sin. What does sin produce? Death. But what does partaking of the divine nature produce? The ability to live free from sin.

Glory to God, we can escape sin and corruption by taking God's escape route. God is giving us a personal access road. And by being born again and regularly partaking of God's divine nature, we can literally escape the corruption of sin. By knowing who we are in Christ and by understanding that the new divine nature is in us, we can resist temptation.

It's so important that every Christian understands the amazing, supernatural equipment that he or she receives in the new nature. It's life changing, and it's an important part of our escape theology. The whole point is that in order to rule and reign over our flesh, we must understand the equipment we have. We must understand who we are in Jesus Christ. We must understand that Jesus Christ has made us brand new.

BRAND NEW YOU

There are, biblically speaking, only two races of people or two families on earth. Each of us is either in God's family or the devil's family. Those are the only two choices, and we're either in one or the other.

Once you choose your family, your father is decided for you. If you're born again, then God is your Father, and you have God's nature or Spirit on the inside of you. If you are not born again and have not accepted Jesus as your Savior, then you have the nature or spirit of this fallen world, and you are fathered by the father of lies, the devil.

Until we are born again as a new creation alive unto God, we are by nature sinners. Our nature before Jesus Christ craved sin; it yielded freely to the lust of our flesh without thought or hesitation; our nature was in full agreement with our flesh.

Yet, as we discussed earlier, every human being is a three-part creation. You are a spirit created after God's own Spirit and that part of you will never cease; that part of you will spend eternity in either heaven or hell. Your spirit is the real you. The second part of you is your soul realm, which is a combination of your mind, your will and your emotions. This realm is where decisions are made and emotions are felt. The third part of your makeup is your body or the flesh house in which you live. Someday when your spirit goes to heaven, your body will return to dust.

But the minute you receive Jesus Christ, your spirit is reborn and your nature changes. Second Corinthians 5:17 says, "Therefore, if anyone *is* in Christ, *he is* a new creation; old things have passed away; behold, all things have become new" (NKJV). You are a new creation, someone who has never existed before, created with the nature of God. It is like putting us back the way God originally intended us to be in the Garden of Eden before man fell.

Before we were born again, our conduct was a result of our fallen nature and our flesh cooperated with our fallen nature; we really had no choice but to live in sin. It makes it easy to understand why sinners are busy sinning. It is their legacy, their heritage, their very nature. Bottom line: Sinners sin.

PIGS DO WHAT PIGS DO

This fact reminds me of a simple—yet profound—lesson I learned growing up on a farm. Here it is: You can put a dress on a pig, but a pig is still a pig. Frankly, the pig wouldn't care if it wore a dress. It would still do what pigs do. If you turned that pig loose, it would wallow in the mud. If there's mud anywhere around, the pig will find it. Why? That's what pigs do. That's who pigs are, and that's what they're all about.

In the same way, the nature of someone who is not born again is the nature of a sinner. We can dress the person up with religion, laws, rules and regulations, and any other thing you can think of, but as soon as the person can, he or she will sin. Why? Because the person is a sinner, and a sinner by any other name is still a sinner who sins.

Based on what we read earlier from Ephesians 2:3, we could say it this way: our sinful behavior was a manifestation of our nature. Because we were not born of God, we were controlled by our sinful nature and in line for God's wrath.

First Peter 2:11 says, "...I implore you as aliens and strangers and exiles [in this world] to abstain from the sensual urges (the evil desires, the passions of the flesh, your lower nature) that wage war against the soul" (AMP). You can see again that the sensual urges come from what this verse calls your lower nature. The lower nature is not born of the Spirit of God. So the only way to get rid of the lower nature or the sensual nature is to trade it in for a new nature or get born again.

It's futile to try to clean up the old nature. That's like putting a dress on a pig. It doesn't work; it never works. Instead, we should allow God to remove the old nature and give us a new one.

The New Testament in Modern English translation of 2 Corinthians 5:17, which we read earlier, says, "...If a man is in Christ he becomes a new person altogether—the past is finished and gone, everything has become fresh and new." The old person is gone, done away with forever. The old person who was a sinner, whose nature was to sin, has died. Goodbye. So long. Don't let the door hit you on the way out.

After you're born again, the old person who had a lower, sensual nature becomes fresh and new, someone who never existed before. You are a new creation, a brand-new you. What an ultimate new beginning. According to 2 Corinthians 5:21, the born-again person is made righteousness with a nature created in God's likeness and His image and is free to live out the new nature free from sin.

It's plain to see from God's Word that only born-again people can really live a lifestyle free from sin. The only way to have a chance to really say no to sin is to receive this new reborn nature and understand it and walk in it.

Sadly, there are a lot of born-again people who still struggle with sin. They don't want to sin, but they do. They try to overcome sin, but they fail. They wring their hands and shed buckets of tears, but they still give way to sin. They try to fight the devil, but they come up empty. They hurt loved ones, and damage relationships, but they cannot seem to help it. They dislike themselves, and they feel powerless.

But God has the solution.

God says you can break free, stay free and live free.

God is all about freedom, and it all begins by understanding who you are in Christ Jesus. When you were born again, something very radical happened to you. *There was a funeral and a resurrection all together in a moment of time.*

The old you died and a new you was resurrected. Don't go back now and try to live like you did before. Unfortunately, it's possible for a Christian who's been given a new nature to live like the devil, live like he or she never received a new nature at all. Some folks bury the new man, never learning about their new nature. They say silly things and believe silly things like, "I'm just a sinner saved by grace."

But if you are a born-again Christian, you were once a sinner, but no longer. You were saved by grace, and thank God for His amazing grace. Now the old you is dead, and now you have been made the righteous of God in Christ Jesus.

So now that you're born again, get out of sin and get out of the mud. Don't stay in that place of thinking that you're still a sinner or a reformed sinner or any kind of sinner. Get away from sin altogether. The Spirit of Grace changes you into a saint, a born-again child of God who is no longer given to sin.

It sounds religious and humble to say, "I am a sinner saved by grace." But really that phrase is not accurate, it's not true and it's not Bible. It's a phrase inspired of the devil through the tradition of men to keep you bound to the old nature. Promise yourself never to use that tired old phrase again. In fact, promise to let your new nature dominate your life.

NEW CLOTHES

It's time to walk and talk different like the new creations we are. We've all noticed that it's easy to be different in church and say amen and smile and nod, but how can we walk the walk and talk the talk 24/7?

It's simple. We put on new clothes.

The new nature is the doorway to your freedom. Even then, you must choose to walk on in the freedom that your new nature provides. Ephesians 4 tells us below to put on this new nature:

> **Ephesians 4:22-24 (NKJV)**
> 22 That you put off, concerning your former conduct, the old man which grows corrupt according to the deceitful lusts,
>
> 23 and be renewed in the spirit of your mind,

> 24 and that you put on the new man which was created according to God, in true righteousness and holiness.

We put on our new nature just like a person puts on a sweater or a jacket. We are to clothe ourselves with the Lord by putting on His ways, His words, His actions and His manner of living. When we are clothed with His presence—living by His Words and walking in His Spirit—we will have no room for any other desires. The lust of our flesh will not have a chance.

Let's look at how The Amplified Bible clarifies these verses even more:

> **Ephesians 4:22-24 (AMP)**
> 22 Strip yourselves of your former nature [put off and discard your old unrenewed self] which characterized your previous manner of life and becomes corrupt through lusts and desires that spring from delusion;
>
> 23 And be constantly renewed in the spirit of your mind [having a fresh mental and spiritual attitude],
>
> 24 And put on the new nature (the regenerate self) created in God's image, [Godlike] in true righteousness and holiness.

Inspired by the Holy Spirit, the apostle Paul instructs believers to take off something—the old you. He tells you to get rid of the old you that existed before you were born again who tolerated deceitful lusts. Paul says to strip off your former nature. I like these descriptive phrases because I get a mental picture of tossing something away – getting rid of it and discarding it like an old flat tire. What do we do with this former, sinful, lustful, deceptive, delusional self? Get it off and get rid of it!

Then verse 24 says to get dressed in your new clothes, in your new nature in God's image. Did you notice that *you must dress yourself in your new clothes?* In other words, they don't just appear automatically.

How do you *put on* a coat? You do it on purpose. You don't accidentally put on your coat; you choose to put it on because it's a covering and a protection from troublesome elements. Likewise, you must put on your new nature because it's a covering and a protection from troublesome sin.

Colossians 3 encourages us with these words:

> **Colossians 3:9-10 (AMP)**
> 9 Do not lie to one another, for you have stripped off the old (unregenerate) self with its evil practices,
>
> 10 And have clothed yourselves with the new [spiritual self], which is [ever in the process of being] renewed and remolded into [fuller and more perfect knowledge upon] knowledge after the image (the likeness) of Him Who created it.

There's no need for us to try and cover the old person with the new person. Instead, we should take the old dead stuff off and just throw it away. Don't save it. Get rid of it. Trash it. Burn it. Then right after you take off those filthy rags, put on that new robe of righteousness that's guaranteed to be a perfect fit. You are to wear new clothes in the spirit, which positions you to speak up and say, "Sin—I don't want to, and I don't have to."

Do you realize that you don't even have to go shopping for these new clothes? There's no browsing store aisles and no waiting in line. These clothes of righteousness are delivered to you by the Holy Spirit.

Notice the instructions in the following scripture:

> **Romans 13:14 (AMP)**
> But clothe yourself with the Lord Jesus Christ (the Messiah), and make no provision

for [indulging] the flesh [put a stop to thinking about the evil cravings of your physical nature] to [gratify its] desires (lusts).

I personally like new clothes, and I like to buy new clothes and apparently so does God because He tells us in His Word to put on something new. His Word tells us to take off the old and put on the new. Notice He never tells us to put the new over the old.

Remember, your spirit or inner man of the heart was born again, but your flesh did not get born again. Those lustful cravings are still there. The same sort of things that tried to get a hold of you and tempt you before you were saved still want to get a hold of you now. That's why you must cooperate with the new nature you received when you became a child of God. You must now partake of the divine nature that is on the inside of you, stripping off sin and putting on righteousness. Then and only then will you be able to truly go and sin no more.

We've looked at Ephesians 2:3, which explained man's sinful nature of wanting to sin and follow after lusts, but let's pinpoint the source of that nature. Where did it come from?

As we discussed in Chapter 2, when Adam and Eve sinned and committed high treason, they fell from grace and could no longer partake of God's nature. Their sin separated them from God, and they no longer could fellowship with Him. But I'm so glad that God had a plan to restore mankind back to Himself. God sent Jesus to pay the price for man's sin, and through Jesus' death, burial and resurrection we can now be restored to God. Jesus has provided salvation for all; His work is finished. Now you and I must choose to receive the forgiveness He purchased for us. It's not automatic to all, but it's available to all.

Someone might say, "If Adam and Eve sinned with God's divine nature inside of them, what hope do I have? Do you think I can succeed where they failed?" You bet I do. For one thing, you have a choice! Just because Adam and Eve made the wrong choice, doesn't mean you have to crash and burn, too.

God has given you His personal manual called the Bible to help you succeed in this life. If you're born again, you have precious promises to help you partake of the divine nature and put on new clothes. You also have the Spirit of God leading and guiding you to victory.

So take out the trash and dispose of the garbage in your life, and you will then put on your supernatural self, created in God's image. You will dump the trash and bring in the treasure. How often will you do this? Every single day. Every day the trash of this world tries to push out your treasure, so every day you must decide what stays in and what goes out. You must refuse to let the old person dominate you and use God's Word to put on the new person every chance you get because this new person will help you live free from sin.

Colossians 3 tells us exactly how the new man or woman will look in the next few verses.

> **Colossians 3:10, 12-14 (NKJV)**
> 10 ...Put on the new man who is renewed in knowledge according to the image of Him who created him.
>
> 12 Therefore, as *the* elect of God, holy and beloved, put on tender mercies, kindness, humility, meekness, longsuffering;
>
> 13 bearing with one another, and forgiving one another, if anyone has a complaint against another; even as Christ forgave you, so you also *must do*.
>
> 14 But above all these things put on love, which is the bond of perfection.

We have to take off the old and put on the new—never trying to put the new over the old. If you were to put on your work clothes over stinky gym clothes or greasy work clothes, would you be clothed properly? No; the filth and grime of the old would contaminate the new clean clothes. You wouldn't want to put up with the stink that would come through, and in just the same way, you have to become a new creation first and then you are ready to put on the man.

Again, how do you put these spiritual clothes on? The key words in verse 10 are *knowledge* and *image*. Where do we find God's knowledge? In the Word of God. Where do we get the correct image of ourselves? In the mirror. What is the mirror? James 1:23 compares the Word of God to a mirror—a supernatural mirror that reflects back who you should be. Take a good long look in the mirror of God's Word and see if the correct reflection stares back at you.

We put on the new nature by being born again, and then the Word of God shows us exactly what we should look like. We've been made righteous and holy, and it's not what we're trying to become but who we really are. After all, we cannot look into the perfect law of liberty—the mirror of God's Word—to see a sinner. We are changed by a new nature and created in the image of God. We put on this new nature like a shirt or a coat. Only in the realm of the spirit can we dress ourselves with what we believe in our heart and say with our mouth.

The Bible is clear. You and I have been given a new nature, God's very own nature, and now God is asking us to dress accordingly. We're supposed to clothe ourselves in the new nature because God wants us to know that we are more than simply forgiven. God wants us walking, talking and dressing like the children of God we are.

Colossians 3:9-10 in The Message Bible says, "...You're done with that old life. It's like a filthy set of ill-fitting clothes you've stripped off and put in the fire. Now you're dressed in a new wardrobe. Every item of your new way of life is custom-made by the Creator, with his label on it. All the old fashions are now obsolete."

DEAD MEN WALKING

After we've changed clothes, Colossians 3 tells us where to direct our attention.

Colossians 3:1-3 (NKJV)
1 If then you were raised with Christ, seek those things which are above, where Christ is, sitting at the right hand of God.

2 Set your mind on things above, not on things on the earth.

3 For you died, and your life is hidden with Christ in God.

How do we accomplish this? We seek those things that are above and set our affection on Him, setting out to please Him in all ways. We run every decision by and through the Word of God and prayer. We don't decide about everything else in our lives and then try to make room for God, nor should we arrange our whole lives and then ask for God's blessing. Our heart and its desires must be turned toward God, not the things of this earth. The things of this earth are no longer our priority because God is No. 1 in our lives.

Then here's the big one: We consider ourselves dead because dead men don't sin. "But wait," someone might ask, "Do you mean *dead* like really *dead*?" By *dead* I mean that the old you is dead, and the new and improved you lives a life hid with God in Christ. Your old dreams and desires are dead, and you've picked up God's dreams and desires for your life, which are bigger and better in every way than anything you could dream up yourself.

Determine that the old you is dead. Go ahead and put up a tombstone and take flowers to the gravesite. Don't go back. Don't look back. There's not much to go back to the way I look at it. The old man is dead, and now there is a divine, full-of-God new person in you ready to live free from sin.

CHAPTER 5

YOU'RE THE BOSS

There's no question that sin involves a three-part equation of the devil, the temptation and *you*. But you make the choices. You call the shots. The devil may line up some tempting scenes along the way, but you are the one who must become the boss of your flesh that's determined to have its own way.

When temptation comes along, you cannot just say, "The devil made me do it!" like 1970s comedian Flip Wilson. The comic used to jokingly blame the devil whenever he got in trouble or did something wrong. It's funny, but it's not true. The truth is that the devil isn't strong enough to make you do anything.

We all know that the devil is happy to suggest a variety of sins to you. He wants to get you out of the will of God every which way he can. The devil does his best to keep up his part of John 10:10, which is to steal, kill and destroy. So make no mistake about it, the devil is out to destroy your life. Worse yet, sin is one of his favorite weapons, which he talks Christians into using on themselves.

He doesn't play around. If he could destroy your family, he would love to do it. If he could destroy your body, he would love to do it. Sometimes the devil attacks just because he's the devil, but we sure don't want to give him any open doors of access in our lives. We need to keep all doors closed.

But while the devil is doing his best to set you up and ruin your life, he cannot pull it off without your help. Jesus defeated the devil, and his only weapon is tempting and persuading you to sin.

Sin is a choice. Sin is *your* choice.

Let's face it. The flesh all by itself craves things that cause a heap of trouble. The flesh craves to get even with people and have revenge. The flesh loves to gossip. The flesh loves to cheat. The flesh loves to eat. The flesh loves to lie. The flesh loves to be lazy. The flesh wants to get away with a whole lot of stuff, but we need to understand how our flesh operates and refuse to let it run the show. God is available 24/7 to help us, but we must choose not to sin. We must crucify our flesh and show it who is boss.

CRAVINGS OF THE FLESH

As long as you're on this earth, you'll obviously be in a body, and as long as you're in a body, it will crave things that can get you in trouble. In fact, through the years I've watched new Christians leave themselves wide open for trouble because they didn't understand this fact.

As a pastor, I've had new believers say to me, "I thought I was saved. I got filled with the Holy Ghost, and yet, I still want to sin. I don't understand why I want to do the same things I used to do." A lot of times these folks believe they're trapped by lusts and desires. But that's a lie!

Remember what Jesus told the woman caught in adultery? He said "I don't condemn you. Now go and sin no more." If Jesus were talking to us today, He would say, "I don't condemn you for your past failures and mistakes, but this is what I would like. I would like for you to learn how to live in victory and not sin anymore."

After all, can any of us lift our hands and say, "I've made it through my whole Christian life without sin?" Of course not. Every Christian needs 1 John 1:9, which says, "If we confess our sins, he is faithful and just to forgive us our sins, and to cleanse us from all unrighteousness." This scripture wouldn't be necessary if Christians didn't sin. But 1 John 1:9 is very necessary because we have all missed the mark. We have all been tempted. We have all sinned. But we all have an advocate with the Father, and we all have the benefit of Jesus Christ paying the price for our sins and shedding His blood to wash them away. Let's looks at several scriptures that will help you gain mastery of your flesh and its cravings.

HOW YOUR BODY OPERATES

In Ephesians 2 we see an important scripture regarding how to control the flesh. Keep in mind that since this scripture is found in Ephesians, it's among the Epistles or letters written to the church at Ephesus as well as to Christians today.

> **Ephesians 2:3 (AMP)**
> Among these we as well as you once lived *and* conducted ourselves in the passions of our flesh [our behavior governed by our corrupt and sensual nature], obeying the impulses of the flesh and the thoughts of the mind [our cravings dictated by our senses and our dark imaginings]. We were then by nature children of [God's] wrath and heirs of [his] indignation, like the rest of mankind.

This scripture confirms again that no Christian is beyond sin or temptation. If you don't think your flesh has impulses, you're kidding yourself. If you don't think your flesh has impulses, you're identifying part of the reason you have trouble conquering them. To overcome temptation and sin, you cannot live in denial. Temptation and sin must be faced head on.

Many born-again Christians still live according to the desires of their flesh because too many don't know how to do it any other way. Yet, God's Word gives us clear and practical teaching that will help us live by our born-again nature and sin no more. In fact, *getting your flesh under control in any area has a lot to do with you walking in victory over sin in every area.*

Just because you are a believer does not mean you will automatically walk free from sin. As long as you live on this earth, your soul and your flesh will have human appetites and desires all their own. That's why you must rule over your flesh. If you don't, then you will give up and say, "I cannot walk with God. I am a sinner."

The devil will spend all day long trying to get you to give in to sinful impulses. Why? So you will get into sin. Why? Because the devil wants you to feel condemned. Why? Because he wants you to throw up your hands in disgust with yourself and give up. This is the devil's plan, and he is a master at getting it done.

But you no longer have to fall prey to the enemy's lies. First Peter 4:2 says "…no longer spend the rest of his natural life living by [his] human appetites *and* desires, but [he lives] for what God wills" (AMP). That's good news! God says we no longer have to spend the rest of our lives giving into our fleshly desires. Listen, the more you learn about freedom from human appetites and desires, the freer you will become and the sweeter your walk with God will be.

So many people get frustrated because they seem to commit the same sins over and over again, until they finally give up and say, "I cannot serve God." Then the devil wins, and the person loses. But if the Lord were standing right in front of you—and He's actually a lot closer than that in a Christian's life—He would say to you, "Neither do I condemn you. Go and sin no more." Yet, the go and sin no more part is what trips a lot of people up.

God doesn't want you tripped up or living in guilt. Still, you are the one who decides whether or not you will live in victory over sin. It's a sad, defeated and carnal walk for a Christian to choose a life of sin, but it's possible for a born-again Christian who's filled with the Holy Spirit to still live in sin for the rest of his or her natural life following after human appetites. In reality a carnal Christian is simply a natural person who has supernatural help lying dormant.

"Isn't that pretty normal?" someone might ask. Yes, and that's exactly the problem. Paul wrote to the Corinthians and said, carnal Christians or "mere unchanged men" (1 Corinthians 3:3 AMP). In other words, Paul was explaining that the Corinthians had chosen to live as mere men instead of living the supernaturally empowered lives God intended. They had chosen to live by the dictates of their flesh. What a miserable life.

Worse yet, sin is a dead-end road. Dead end is exactly what it will be because Romans 8:6 says that to be carnally minded is death. Sin always results in a paycheck of death. Sin may not instantly produce physical death, but it produces death just the same. Sin in a marriage could cause the death of a marriage. Cheating or stealing at work can cause the death of employment. Lying about a friend or spreading gossip could cause the death of a friendship. And the list goes on and on.

That's why Peter says by the Holy Spirit that we should not spend the rest of our natural lives living by our human appetites. In today's language, we might say, don't live by your stinkin' carnal flesh; let your spirit man dominate. If you live by the dictates of your body and soul, your motto will be whatever feels good, do it; whatever seems right, try it. It's a body and soul gone wild.

Sometimes Christians say, "Oh, I could never go wild and sin." But they turn their body loose all the time. If their body wants to be late for work, they hit the snooze button. "Aw, that's all right. I'll get another job. I've got six sick days left, and I've got to use them," the person might say. The trouble is, if you start yielding to your flesh like that, it opens the door for many things. You've got to keep your body under control or it will put you under.

"Pastor Mark, I could never do that! I've got to have my morning coffee lest I tear up everybody I meet." Really? Then coffee has dominion over you. Think about it. We all have our own issues, and we all have to put the flesh down.

Yet, one thing is clear. If you're reading this book, then you don't want to yield to your flesh. You don't want the devil to win, so you must keep your flesh in line. The first step to winning over sin is to own the fact that you have human appetites that need to be put under and controlled. Every single one of us has cravings of the flesh to put down—no exceptions. And no Christian—no person—can fix a problem that he or she won't admit to having.

When anyone of us lets his or her body do whatever it wants to do, say whatever it wants to say, the door to trouble is wide open. "Yeah, but I just have to say what's on my mind," someone might say. Actually, no, you don't. If you're always saying what's on your mind, then you're yielding to your flesh because no one's thoughts are always holy, pure, peaceable, lovely, kind, gentle and long-suffering. Maybe you need to find your delete button and hit it more often.

If what's on your mind doesn't agree with God's Word, don't think it, let alone say it. Galatians 5:16 says, "...Walk in the Spirit, and you shall not fulfill the lust of the flesh" (NKJV). And if you don't walk in the Spirit, then what happens? Then you will give way to the lusts of the flesh and fulfill the appetites of the flesh morning, noon and night.

First John 3:6 gives us good advice and says, "No one who abides in Him [who lives and remains in communion with and in obedience to Him—*deliberately, knowingly, and habitually] commits [practices] sin*. No one who [*habitually*] sins has either seen or knows Him [recognized, perceived, or understood Him, or has had an experiential acquaintance with Him]" (AMP). This scripture is as clear as can be. It makes the point that no one who deliberately, knowingly and habitually practices sin really knows Him. Isn't this true? It is. Believers should not practice sin; believers should not live in sin. Period.

Another scripture that will nail this down for us is Galatians 5:21, which says, "That they which do such things [sin] shall not inherit the kingdom of God." The words *do such things* come from the original Greek word *prasso*, which is literally translated *"those who put these things into practice in their lives and do these things routinely as a manner of lifestyle shall not enter the kingdom of God."*

There's a big difference between committing sin in a single instance and practicing sin as a lifestyle. One instance of sin can be a result of poor choices, impulsive behavior or losing control of one's sense. But practicing sin is willful, deliberate and premeditated. The Bible is saying that we may occasionally miss the mark and sin, and for that 1 John 1:9 is our solution. But you and I must understand that there's no excuse for living in sin day in and day out.

Let's read the maintenance scripture for Christians in 1 John 1; it will keep us in right standing with God.

> **1 John 1:8-10**
> 8 If we say that we have no sin, we deceive ourselves, and the truth is not in us.
> 9 If we confess our sins, he is faithful and just to forgive us our sins and to cleanse us from all unrighteousness.

10 If we say that we have not sinned, we make him a liar, and his word is not in us.

Notice that both verses 8 and 10 make it clear that even as Christians, we still sin. After all, the epistle of 1 John was written to Christians. Then in 1 John 2:1 the Bible says, "My little children, these things write I unto you, that ye sin not, And if any man sin, we have an advocate with the Father, Jesus Christ the righteous." The scripture is talking to Christians because it reads "my little children." The Bible is telling us that it's the will of God that you don't sin, but if you sin, there's help available. If you sin, you have an advocate in Jesus, who will be your lawyer.

But does that mean that we should sin 101 times a day and confess our sins 101 times a day and then do it all over again the next day? No. While God is full of infinite mercy and forgiveness, the solution is to take control of our flesh and put an end to the practice of sin.

TAKING CONTROL

Let's look at a scripture that will help us face the problem of the flesh head on and take control.

Romans 6:12 says, "Let not sin therefore reign in your mortal body, that ye should obey it in the lusts thereof." The verse is telling us that sin doesn't have to reign in our bodies, and we don't have to obey our fleshly lusts. Now it doesn't say that you don't lust, and it doesn't say to ignore lust. Actually, to simply ignore the fact that your flesh has unholy desires is very dangerous. The main point of this scripture is that we don't have to allow sin to rule and reign in our bodies; we don't have to obey the lusts.

As we've discussed in previous chapters, our spirit was reborn at the new birth, but our bodies and our minds still need work. Even though we become born again and our sinful nature is replaced with a divine nature, our soul must be renewed. Our soul must be cleaned up and trained to live a new and different way. For a lot of people that means having a "come to Jesus meeting" to get their will lined up with His.

Jesus Himself went to the Garden of Gethsemane and told the Father, "Not my will but Yours be done." If Jesus had to commit His will to the Father, we will probably have to commit ours on a regular basis. But while our spirit is reborn and our soul is renewed, our flesh needs to be controlled.

Let me remind you of a scripture that really helped start me along this entire journey. Galatians 5:16 says, "…Walk in the Spirit, and you shall not fulfill the lust of the flesh" (NKJV). If you walk in the Spirit, and are more aware of spiritual things than natural things, you will not fulfill the desires of your flesh. Make no mistake about it, your flesh has desires and most are not godly. If you don't walk in the Spirit that means you will walk by the dictates of your flesh, and those same fleshly cravings will lead you right back into the sin and misery that bound you in the first place. So what do you do with your flesh?

Kill it!

Of course I don't mean that you literally kill your flesh, but you kill it metaphorically. In other words, you subdue it.

Control it.

Rule over it.

Boss it around.

If you don't boss your flesh around, it will boss you around. If you don't kill your flesh, it will kill you, for the paycheck of sin is ultimately death.

The sum total of how to handle your flesh is found in one word: No! Just say no.

If you want to live free from sin and its effects, you'll have to tell your flesh no. And you'll have to tell it no on a regular and continual basis.

Colossians 3:5 says, "So kill (deaden, deprive of power) the evil lurking in your members…" (AMP). When we say *kill*, we're talking about depriving our flesh of the right to rule and reign in our lives. Crucifying the flesh sounds painful, and it is. But it sure beats the penalty of death carried by sin.

"Yeah, but, wasn't Jesus crucified so I don't have to be?" someone might ask. Jesus was crucified to pay the penalty for your sin, but you still need to discipline your flesh and keep your body under. Even the great apostle Paul had to deal with his flesh. Notice how he got the job done. He said, "…I discipline my body and bring *it* into subjection, lest, when I have preached to others, I myself should become disqualified" (1 Corinthians 9:27 NKJV). Notice how The Amplified Bible translates this verse, "…Like a boxer I buffet my body [handle it roughly, discipline it by hardships] and subdue it. …"

"But, Mark, I thought you said this was all going to be easy?" It is easy. You don't have to discipline and control your flesh on your own. You've got help!

"Yeah but, I just cannot control my flesh. I've tried. I don't have enough willpower." I'm not talking about you ruling over your body with willpower; I'm talking about you ruling over your body with God power. I'm talking about you walking in the Spirit—empowered by the Spirit of God—and walking according to the power of God's Word to put you over in this life.

"Shouldn't there be like a line at church where the pastor prays and our bodies just want to do right after that?" I wish that were true, but it isn't.

Nevertheless, the Bible says in 1 Thessalonians 4:4, "Every one of you should know how to possess his vessel [body] in sanctification and honour." And since the Bible told us we *should* know how to possess our vessel, then we *can* possess our vessel. That's the bottom line.

THE PANGS OF SACRIFICE

Practically speaking, how do we possess our vessels or our bodies? How do we take control? The Bible tells us to present our bodies as a living sacrifice.

Romans 12:1 says, "I beseech you therefore, brethren, by the mercies of God, that ye present your bodies a living sacrifice, holy, acceptable unto God, which is your reasonable service." You and I are to bring our body like a sacrificial lamb or an offering before the Lord and give it to Him for His use, His honor, His glory.

To just let our flesh do whatever it wants sets us up for failure. If we let sin rule in our bodies, we will obey lusts. So what do we do? We must refuse to let sin rule. We must pick up our flesh and haul it to the altar and lay it down. We must present our flesh as a living sacrifice and tell the flesh that it won't be having its way anymore. We must tell our body that a new day has dawned and our regenerated, reborn, redeemed blood-bought spirit is calling the shots from here on out. And then we make ourselves walk on in the Spirit.

Rhonda teaches that the only problem with a living sacrifice is that it's always trying to get off the altar and walk away. That's why you have to put your flesh in its place on the altar and keep it there.

Romans 6 tells us that a living sacrifice that remains on the altar must yield its body as an instrument of righteousness.

> **Romans 6:12-13:**
> 12 Let not sin therefore reign in your mortal body, that ye should obey it in the lusts thereof.
>
> 13 Neither yield ye your members as instruments of unrighteousness unto sin: but yield yourselves unto God, as those that are alive from the dead, and your members as instruments of righteousness unto God.

Offering our bodies as a living sacrifice *is* our reasonable service. After all, our bodies are now the temple of the Holy Spirit. When we have a revelation of 1 Corinthians 3:16 and 6:19 and understand that our bodies carry around the presence of God, then we will keep our temples holy. The Bible says we have a treasure in our earthen vessels, and we are carriers of the glory of God.

Let me give you a number of reasons why you should keep your flesh under and a list of ways to do it. In fact, notice how Peter teaches us.

> **1 Peter 4:1-2 (AMP)**
> 1 So, since Christ suffered in the flesh for us, for you, arm yourselves with the same thought and purpose [patiently to suffer rather than fail to please God]. For whoever has suffered in the flesh [having the mind of Christ] is done with [intentional] sin [has stopped pleasing himself and the world, and pleases God].
>
> 2 So that he can no longer spend the rest of his natural life living by [his] human appetites and desires, but [he lives] for what God wills.

This scripture brings to light two important points to help keep our bodies under. It points out that some suffering may be required to stop sin, and it points out that we must stop living to please ourselves.

The New Living Translation says:

> **1 Peter 4:1-2**
> 1 So then, since Christ suffered physical pain, you must arm yourselves with the same attitude he had, and be ready to suffer, too. For if you have suffered physically for Christ, you have finished with sin.
>
> 2 You won't spend the rest of your lives chasing your own desires, but you will be

anxious to do the will of God.

Does this mean that you are expected to fly to Golgatha, erect a cross and suffer as Jesus did on the cross? No, but it does mean that you will have to tell your flesh no from time to time and suffer the pangs that come from denying your flesh something it wants.

Look at yet another modern-day translation of this verse from The Message.

> **1 Peter 4:1-2**
> 1 Since Jesus went through everything you're going through and more, learn to think like him. Think of your sufferings as a weaning from that old sinful habit of always expecting to get your own way.
>
> 2 Then you'll be able to live out your days free to pursue what God wants instead of being tyrannized by what you want.

Do you see the heart change that will drive sin far away from you? To get victory over sin, first and foremost, you must put what God wants ahead of what you want. If it's painful, then think of your "sufferings as a weaning from that old sinful habit of always expecting to get your own way." "Arm yourself with the same attitude" Jesus had, and in doing so you will no longer please yourself.

The truth is, the will of God will oppose our flesh today, tomorrow and forever. It will oppose the flesh in big things and small things no matter who we are. But by doing the will of God, the by-product will be that our flesh becomes trained to walk in line with God's Word.

How do you train your flesh? Usually it means going against what feels good to a lazy, old body. For instance, the Bible says to forsake not the assembling of yourselves together (Hebrews 10:25). So, when it's time to go to church, you go whether you feel like it or not. Your flesh may say, "I don't want to. I'm busy. I'm tired." But you tell your flesh, "So what? You're going anyway! When the church doors are open, that's where a Christian belongs!"

Then when you get to church, it's time to praise and worship God. Your flesh may say, "But what if I don't want to sing? What if I don't like the songs? What if the drums are too loud? What if I don't want to stand?" You tell your flesh, "So what? You're doing it anyway. I'm here to worship God, and I tell you what to do!"

Here's a good one. What about when the offering bucket comes along, and it's time to give back to the Lord your tithe or 10 percent of your income (Malachi 3). What if you don't want to? What if you need some extra cash? You do it anyway. And in this way, you are training your flesh to do the will of God. You are putting God's will and God's Word above your wants and your desires, so that sin cannot have dominion in your flesh.

If you regularly tell your flesh what to do in these areas, then your flesh will know who is boss when it comes to bigger things. *Don't wait to put your flesh under at a crisis point; keep your flesh under all the time.* The devil looks for the lusts of your flesh, and when he finds them, he tempts them. But if you keep your flesh under, when the devil comes along he will have nothing to work with in your life.

Another way to keep our flesh under is through reverence. Consider this scripture.

> **2 Corinthians 7:1**
> Having therefore these promises, dearly beloved, let us cleanse ourselves from all filthiness of the flesh and spirit, perfecting holiness in the fear of God.

Don't let the word *holiness* scare you. Acting holy is nothing spooky or weird; it's just living. It's living like Jesus did when He was on this earth. We could also say that reverencing God is having a reverential fear of God.

Does that mean we're supposed to be afraid of God? Of course not. A fear of God is having an awesome respect for God, for who He is and what He has done. When we reverence God, it will help us cleanse ourselves from the filth of the flesh. As we exalt God to first place in our lives, fleshy things fall by the wayside.

THE WAR IN THE SOUL

Let's look at another scripture that talks about the war that lust creates in our soul. First Peter 2:11 says, "Dearly beloved, I beseech you as strangers and pilgrims, abstain from fleshly lusts, which war against the soul."

I want to quote this passage from *Sparkling Gems from the Greek*, written by one of my favorite authors, Rick Renner. Here he uses various words to amplify the meaning of 1 Peter 2:11.

> Dearly beloved, I sincerely beg and warn you to live as if you are travelers here in this world. Never forget that this is not your real residence and that you must not become too attached to the environment around you. I urge you to refrain from any carnal, low-level desires that try to engulf you and thus drag you into a very long, protracted, strategic, and aggressive war in your mind, will, and emotions.

More than any other generation that's ever lived on the earth, we face more temptation to our eyes and ears than ever before. It's everywhere—television, movies, print media, Internet, billboards on the streets, at school and at work. Everywhere we confront words and pictures and messages that in times past no one could even have imagined would be posted in public forums. And the devil knows it. The devil is smart enough to realize that temptation enters your heart through your eyes and ears and chokes out God's Word.

I'm not about to preach you a "clothesline sermon" and tell you to throw out your television or never read another magazine again. I'm not saying disconnect the Internet, but I am saying you've got to understand how the enemy works. He's out to tantalize your flesh anyway he can. And we all know that your flesh wants what it wants and sometimes what it wants isn't so holy.

We're not only talking about sexual sins either. Some people think, *Well at least I'm not committing adultery. At least I'm not fornicating.* OK, but are you worrying? Are you gossiping? Are you overeating? Are you lying? You can try to measure sin all you want, but to God sin is sin.

We all understand that our flesh lusts for things. God understands that, too. But His solution is pretty simple. The Bible tells us to get it under control and show our flesh who is boss.

CHAPTER 6

WALK IN THE SPIRIT AND AWAY FROM SIN

The Bible tells us in Galatians 5 that if we walk in the Spirit, we will not walk in the flesh. That means every step in the Spirit is another step away from sin. And it's the answer to winning over sin. But does walking in the Spirit mean we should walk around with goose bumps in some woo-woo world with our head stuck in the clouds? No. The Bible tells us that walking in the Spirit simply means living a life that's pleasing to our Lord.

Galatians 5:16 in The Amplified Bible puts it this way: "...Walk and live [habitually] in the [Holy] Spirit [*responsive to and controlled and guided by the Spirit*]; then you will certainly not gratify the cravings and desires of the flesh...."

The apostle John gives us more insight when he said he was in the Spirit on the Lord's Day (Revelation 1:10). Does that mean John found a new location somewhere? No. John wasn't talking about a geographical location; he was talking about a spiritual position.

Actually, if you asked 100 people what the phrase *in the Spirit* means, you would probably get 100 different answers. Yet, I believe the best explanation of being in the Spirit is being more aware of spiritual things than natural things.

It doesn't mean you float on a cloud, and it doesn't mean you have an out-of-body experience. If you're a woman, it doesn't mean wearing long flowing gowns and acting like midcentury evangelist Kathryn Kuhlman. If you're a man, it doesn't mean speaking in thees and thous. Walking in the Spirit is literally walking according to the Word and the Spirit and living a life controlled by them.

Of course there are people who say they walk in the Spirit when in reality they are off in some granola club of nuts, fruits and flakes. That's also not what I'm talking about. Walking in the Spirit is walking in the light of God's Word. It makes you a better person not a weird person. It's someone who lives with God's Word as the final authority in life and someone who is really yielded to and in tune with the Holy Spirit.

Walking in the Spirit is not out of the ordinary for a believer; it's what we are supposed to do. Galatians 5:16 refers to it as a daily experience of living out of our spirit, living responsive to the Holy Spirit, letting Him guide and direct us in all the affairs of life.

In fact, a few verses further down in the chapter, Galatians 5:25 tells us, "Since we are living by the Spirit, let us follow the Spirit's leading in every part of our lives" (NLT). For example, if we're walking in the Spirit, we are responsive to the Holy Spirit and when He urges us to do something, we quickly obey.

If the Holy Spirit prompts us to make changes in some areas, we adjust. If the Holy Spirit prompts us to go somewhere or do something, we do it. If He prompts us to pray for someone or call someone or minister to someone, we do. As we read our Bibles and something jumps off the page, we respond to it and put the principle to work in our lives. This means we're not just hearers of the Word of God, but we actually *do it*.

Unfortunately, for some people letting the Holy Spirit control their lives is just a promise they make to God in church when the music is playing softly and the minister asks everyone to promise out loud together. What happens on Monday morning? What happens at work when the Spirit of God deals with you not to accept an invitation to meet up with your colleagues at the bar or to not join in talking trash about the boss?

What happens when you're at home with your spouse and tempted to give him or her a piece of your mind? Do you follow the leading of the Spirit of God in those rubber-meets-the-road moments of life? All those moments count and determine whether or not you live guided by the Spirit of God. It's His job to guide you and me into all truth, and we need to let Him do His job.

Consider this. Have you ever gone on a tour with a knowledgeable guide? A good guide leads you to the best places and helps you get the most out of your tour. A good guide also knows how to help you avoid the pitfalls and traps that will disappoint you and ruin your experience. In the same way, the Holy Spirit is your own personal tour guide through life who knows how to help you stay in the high places and stay out of trouble.

That's why we read in Galatians 5:25, "If we live by the [Holy] Spirit, let us also walk by the Spirit. [If by the Holy Spirit we have our life in God, let us go forward walking in line, our conduct controlled by the Spirit]" (AMP). If our conduct is controlled by the Spirit, then we yield ourselves and our body to Him. After all, our body is the temple or the home of the Holy Spirit (1 Corinthians 6:19).

When you think about it, the Holy Spirit cannot help you with your flesh if He does not live in you. That is why you could never overcome sin on your own and apart from the new birth.

Somebody might say, "I think I can handle this sin thing with the Ten Commandments." Really? I don't think so. God gave us the big ten to let us know we need a Savior. But those of us who have received Jesus Christ as Lord and Savior know that we also need to be controlled, guided and empowered by the Holy Spirit through life.

WHAT IT'S NOT

Sometimes in order to understand something better, we need to consider what it's not. So although we've talked about what walking in the spirit is, let's talk about what it is not or what it looks like to be controlled by your flesh.

Romans 8:5 says, "For those who are according to the flesh and are controlled by its unholy desires set their minds on and pursue those things which gratify the flesh, but those who are according to the Spirit and are controlled by the desires of the Spirit set their minds on and seek those things which gratify the [Holy] Spirit" (AMP).

If someone is flesh driven, the person is not controlled by the Holy Spirit. Why is this important? Because the devil is looking for something in us that he can use to conceive sin, as we mentioned earlier. He is looking for the lust of the flesh that will tempt you to sin. So the more you think about fleshly things and gravitate toward them, the more ammunition you're giving the devil to fire your way.

To be controlled by the flesh means we let our flesh have its way whenever it wants. The thing is, everyone has unholy desires—that includes your minister, Saint Sally, your grandma (oh, yes she does) and the worst sinner you've ever met. The difference lays in what each person does with unholy desires when they come along. The whole point is whether we give in to them or not.

Some people—either on purpose or just by hanging around God a long time—have figured out how to put down their flesh and have learned to let God dominate in their lives. They have learned to pass up marvelous opportunities to sin. They have renewed their minds, and they no longer gratify their flesh.

On the other hand, people who are flesh-ruled do whatever they want whenever they want. Their motto is if it feels good, do it. They live by momentary pleasure and give no thought to the fact that the devil is standing by to conceive with their desires and produce a paycheck of death.

In Romans 8 we get a Holy Spirit lesson on the difference between walking in the flesh and walking in the Spirit that draws a clear line for us to see. Understanding this line is a key to our breaking free and staying free of sin, and if we really want to win over sin, then we must understand this point. Romans 8:13 says, "For if you live according to the flesh you will die; but if by the Spirit you put to death the deeds of the body, you will live" (NKJV). We're talking here about life and death.

Remember the phrase the devil used on Eve? We talked about it in Chapter 2. God had warned Adam and Eve not to eat of a certain fruit or they would die, but when the devil was tempting Eve he said, "Oh, you won't actually die." What a liar! Death came to all mankind because Eve believed that lie. And the devil says the same thing to you all the time.

When he's trying to talk you into a sin, he'll say to you, "You don't think just this once will hurt, do you? Who will find out? What harm could it cause to try it just this once?" Don't believe him! He's such a big liar. He's still the same liar he was back in the Garden of Eden. Sin will cause death in your life; you may not physically die, but make no mistake about it, death in some form will occur.

If something has to die, let it be the deeds of the flesh. After all, the Holy Spirit offered to help you. The Amplified Bible says in

Romans 8:13 ". . . putting to death [making extinct, deadening] the [evil] deeds prompted by the body . . . ."

The desires of your flesh need to die out, and once that happens, you will really start living. The devil may have just whispered to you, "There goes all your fun." But that's another lie! If you think death is fun, then have at it. I know from experience that nothing can measure up to the life God gives. It's full, rich and over-the-top wonderful.

Once you've walked in the Spirit, you'll want to walk there all day long every day. "Why would I want to do that?" someone might ask. The answer is simple. On this earth you're limited by the knowledge and help available here, but if you walk in the Spirit, you walk with all of heaven at your disposal.

Let me quote again from Rick Renner's book, *Sparkling Gems from the Greek,* which talks about walking in the Spirit as our lifestyle. Here he uses various words to convey the idea of Galatians 5:16:

> **Make the path of the Spirit the place where you habitually live and walk. Become so comfortable on this spiritual path that you learn to leisurely and peacefully stroll along in that realm. Living your life in this Spirit realm is the best way to guarantee that you will not allow the yearnings of your flesh to creep out and fulfill themselves.**

WAYS TO WALK IN THE SPIRIT

"Walking in the Spirit sounds amazing, but how do I do it? Is it really hard to do?" someone might ask. It can be as simple as reading and speaking the Word of God and connecting with His presence. John 6:63 quotes Jesus saying, "…the words I speak unto you, they are Spirit, and they are life." When you and I speak His words, they put us in the realm of the Spirit because they are spirit and life.

Another way we can get into the Spirit is to worship God. John 4:24 says, "God is a spirit: and they that worship him must worship him in spirit and in truth." This scripture tells us that we must worship God with truth, which is His Word, and we come to the Father by His Spirit. It's by these avenues that we enter the realm of the spirit.

Someone might say, "The only time I worship is when I'm singing at church." It shouldn't be that way. You can worship with or without music in your home, in your car, at school, at work—really, anywhere you are. God has called you to be a worshipper, and you can magnify and worship God anytime anywhere you want by quietly lifting your voice. Speaking just above a whisper, you can say, "God You're so good." Or "God You're so faithful" and you are worshipping Him.

Worshipping this way connects you with the Spirit of God and you become more aware of God than natural things that surround you. You bring God on the scene in your behalf and it changes your environment.

God offers us many ways to get into the Spirit. Another important way is by being full of the Holy Spirit. The Bible tells us that when a person is born again, they receive the Spirit of God on the inside. Yet, Acts 2 also talks about receiving the baptism of the Holy Spirit, an additional infilling with the evidence of speaking in other tongues.

Acts 1:8 says, "But you shall receive *power* when the Holy Spirit has come upon you…" (NKJV). The word *power* in the Greek is *dunamis*, and it's where we get our word for dynamite and dynamo. In other words, the infilling of the Spirit is power; it's power for service and power for living. No Christian should be without it. Acts 2:4 tells us that the initial evidence of this experience subsequent to salvation is the evidence of speaking in other tongues.

As a pastor, I strongly recommend that every Christian ask for this Holy Spirit infilling. It's the gateway to more of God in your life, and it's the boldness and the backbone to rise above sin.

I've often counseled people, saying, "Try praying in tongues when you're tempted to sin. It will stop you in your tracks." Can you imagine committing adultery while praying in tongues? Of course not, and that's the point.

Or can you imagine singing, "How Great Is Our God" while practicing sin? No. That's the point. The more you are in the Spirit, the less you will yield to your flesh. In the Spirit you will stop practicing and living in sin. You will quit yielding to temptation, and you will be free. You will experience life instead of death, and you will be a person full of joy and victory.

Let's look at walking in the Spirit from one more perspective. If all we speak about are natural things or how we feel about things, we are locked into the natural, physical flesh realm. In turn, the more we're stuck in the flesh realm, the easier it is for us to yield to our flesh. Unfortunately, most people already know the rest of the story. The devil comes along and tempts the flesh with an assortment of lusts and sin is the end result. Yet, if we continue our walk in the Spirit, we resist temptation and live the good life God planned for us. The shackles of sin fall off.

FRUIT TELLS THE STORY

"How can I know if I'm walking in the Spirit?" someone might ask. That's easy. Your fruit tells the story.

Galatians 5 tells us that if we walk by our flesh, we will manifest verse 19 through verse 21, which starts with adultery and ends with revellings. If we walk in the Spirit, we will manifest verses 22 through 23, which include the fruit of the Spirit or love, joy, peace, long-suffering, gentleness, goodness, faithfulness, meekness and temperance.

So it's easy to tell what realm we walk in, and it's easy to walk in the Spirit. God has given us all the same opportunity. It is not something just certain people do at church. It is something we all can do anywhere, anytime, and it determines what our lives produce. Each of us either produces the fruit of the Spirit or the works of the flesh. It's not up to God; it's up to you and me.

Does being filled with the Spirit make you perfect? Of course not. In fact, sometimes people ask crazy questions like, "I heard that Spirit-filled preacher stole $100,000 from his church. Was he in the Spirit?" Obviously he was not full of the Holy Spirit that day. Just because someone spoke in tongues yesterday—or any other day—does not mean the person is immune from yielding to the devil.

Can you prove that? I can. Remember when Peter said, "You're the Lord. You're the Christ. You're the son of the living God." Jesus was pleased with him because he spoke truth that was supernaturally revealed to him. But when Jesus talked about being crucified on the cross, Peter said "Not so!" Jesus turned right around in the same breath and rebuked Peter, saying, "Get behind me Satan!" Peter went from being in the Spirit to in the flesh in a split second (Matthew 16). Can people flip on a dime that quick? Yes.

We need to realize that just because a person has spoken in tongues doesn't mean he or she cannot do wrong. And just because a person is Spirit-filled or has received the baptism of the Holy Spirit does not mean that he or she is always walking in the fullness of the Spirit. Ephesians 5:18 says "…be not drunk with wine, wherein is excess; but be filled with the Spirit." That Greek word filled actually means "be being filled" or continually being *filled*. Bottom line, even people who get filled must get continually refilled in order to stay filled.

Let me put it this way. Christians who walk in the Spirit do pray in other tongues, but not all people who pray in other tongues yield to the Holy Spirit and walk in the Spirit 24 hours a day. Speaking in tongues will help you walk in the Spirit, and it's also the gateway to much more. Walking in the Spirit also means crucifying the flesh and walking by the Word, which requires diligence and discipline.

If you saw the movie "The Passion of the Christ," you saw a graphic crucifixion with lots of blood and gore. You witnessed Jesus suffering pain and anguish in His body as He paid the price for your salvation. That price has been paid in full and is available to all who will believe and receive what Jesus has provided.

And yet, in order to walk in the fullness of salvation Jesus purchased for you, you also are instructed to crucify your flesh and offer your "body as a living sacrifice" (Romans 12:1-2). Are you to hang on a cross? Of course not. But you must die to self. Do you actually die? No. But you must kill off sinful desires, lusts and appetites, and sometimes it's painful.

"That sounds hard, Pastor Mark." Actually, it's not hard at all if you walk in the spirit. I heard a preacher say one time that dead men don't sin. Is it hard for a dead body not to talk back? No. Is it hard for a dead body not to get angry? No. Is it hard for a dead body not to get worked up and agitated in traffic? No. Why? Because dead bodies are *dead*. That's the whole point of being a living sacrifice—your body is dead to sin.

So put your flesh under and keep it under. Put your flesh on the altar and keep it there. If it squirms off the altar for a day, what do you do? Repent and get it right back on the altar. Sure, you'll mess up. We all do. That's what 1 John 1:9 is all about.

"Oh, pastor, this is too hard." Don't be a sissy Christian. Get back up on the altar and let's do this. Let's please God and let's do this to the glory and the honor of God. He's made a way for us out of darkness into light, so let's stay in the light. With His help, you can do anything.

SOW TO THE SPIRIT

All day long, every single day you are confronted with choices that decide whether you walk in the Spirit or in the flesh. Galatians 6 says every choice either sows to the Spirit or to the flesh.

Galatians 6:7-8 (NKJV)
7 Do not be deceived, God is not mocked; for whatever a man sows, that he will also reap.

8 For he who sows to his flesh will of the flesh reap corruption, but he who sows to the Spirit will of the Spirit reap everlasting life

What is sowing to the flesh? It is allowing your flesh to do whatever it wants. What is sowing to the Spirit? It is following after the Word and the Spirit. What's the difference? One reaps life; one reaps death.

Let me give you a practical example. Maybe you want to have the last word in an argument, but you kill that temptation by putting your hand over your mouth. What happens? You've sown to the spirit by lining up your speech with God's Word of love and forgiveness. Sometimes walking in love is simply keeping your mouth shut. That may not sound spiritual, but it can be a very spiritual thing to do.

Consider these situations. Most of the time sexual sins are the first to come to mind on the topic of sin, but there are all kinds of ways to "flesh out." For instance, this is America and nobody likes to talk about overeating even though it's one of the biggest health problems in the country. But the point is that we need to get lusts of every kind under control because if we don't, we open ourselves up to destruction in every area of life. It's a door wide open for the devil. So what if you're staring down a piece of coconut cream pie with meringue about a mile high? Will you sow to the flesh or the Spirit?

What if you're married but an attractive co-worker invites you to lunch? What if you're in charge of the office petty cash box, but you think temporarily borrowing $20 wouldn't be so bad? What if someone undeserving is promoted over you? What if you feel like giving someone a piece of your mind? What will you do in these situations and the situations you face daily? Will you sow to the flesh or sow to the Spirit?

Ephesians 2:10 says, "For we are God's [own] handiwork (His workmanship), recreated in Christ Jesus, [born anew] that we may do those good works which God predestined (planned beforehand) for us [taking paths which He prepared ahead of time], that we should walk in them [***living the good life*** which He prearranged and made ready for us to live]" (AMP). If we want to walk in the good life God has planned for us, then one thing is clear: We must walk in the Spirit and away from sin.

CHAPTER 7
THE BENEFITS OF RIGHTEOUSNESS

Righteousness is a key to living sin free because it has no problem closing the door on sin. An understanding of righteousness will give us a whole new understanding of what Jesus provided for us on the cross and will completely change our position. Righteousness will cause us to realize that we're not looking up at sin as it beats us down, but we're seated in heavenly places with Christ Jesus refusing to sin because it's as under our feet as the devil himself.

Righteousness can be defined as right standing with God or to be right with God, and the Bible calls righteousness a free gift that Jesus provided for all who will receive it. Romans 3:24 in The Amplified Bible says, "[All] are justified and made upright and in right standing with God, freely and gratuitously by His grace (His unmerited favor and mercy), through the redemption which is [provided] in Christ Jesus."

The Message says of the same scripture, "Out of sheer generosity he [God] put us in right standing with himself. A pure gift. He got us out of the mess we're in and restored us to where he always wanted us to be. And he did it by means of Jesus Christ." Thank God, Jesus paid the price for us. Now all we have to do is receive His work and walk in it.

"But I don't feel righteous," a Christian might say. Maybe you don't "feel" righteous, but God's Word says that if you are born again you have received the free gift of righteousness. The New Living Translation of Romans 3:24 says, "Yet God, with undeserved kindness, declares that we are righteous. He did this through Christ Jesus when he freed us from the penalty for our sins." Notice the phrase, "God, with underserved kindness, declares that we are righteous." It's not a matter of how you feel; it's a matter of what Jesus did for you out of the kindness of His heart. If you receive the free gift of righteousness that He's giving you and walk in it, the feelings will come.

Yet, what you really need is a revelation of what you have already received. As I've taught the Word of God to people for more than two decades, I've come to realize that people have a big problem seeing themselves like God does. That's part of the reason that sin is such a big problem even for Christians. But getting a revelation of righteousness will solve both problems. It will cause us to see ourselves as God sees us, and when that happens, sin drops off.

You see, righteousness is not something you do; it's a free gift because of something Jesus has already done for you.

In the beginning there was perfect fellowship between God and Adam and Eve until they disobeyed. When they chose to sin instead of to obey, man fell from grace. The consequences of sin brought death and sin into the earth. But God immediately set a plan into motion to restore mankind back to Himself. He sent Jesus Christ, who was with God in heaven from the beginning, to earth.

God's miraculous plan was for Jesus to be born of a virgin and still be all God and all man all at the same time. Jesus paid the price of man's redemption on the cross so that once again God and man could walk in fellowship. Jesus paid the ultimate price for you and me.

Second Corinthians 5:21 tells us Jesus became sin so that you could be the righteousness of God in Christ Jesus. If you've received Jesus as your Lord and Savior, when God looks at you He no longer sees sin, for the blood of Jesus has washed you clean. He did the work; you reap the benefits.

His righteousness cleanses you from all guilt, from all pain, from all shame, and you can stand clean. It doesn't matter what someone did as a sinner before he or she was born again; the old is gone and done away with. You are a new creation in Christ Jesus.

Jesus restored fellowship between God and those who receive Jesus as Lord. As a child of God, you now have a 24/7 audience with Almighty God. You can go boldly to the throne of grace when and if you sin, where you've got an advocate or lawyer named Jesus who will represent you. I guarantee you that this attorney has never lost a case, and He won't lose yours.

THE FRUIT OF RIGHTEOUSNESS

As we take this gift of righteousness and walk in it every day of our lives, we'll find there's no better way to live. The fruit of righteousness will manifest in so many ways.

1. Your prayers will be powerful and effective.

James 5:16 says, "…The earnest (heartfelt, continued) prayer of a righteous man makes tremendous power available [dynamic in its working]" (AMP). First Peter 3:12 says, "For the eyes of the Lord are over the righteous, and his ears are open unto their prayers: but the face of the Lord is against them that do evil."

You might think to yourself, *I guess I'm not righteous enough because I wouldn't exactly call my prayer life powerful.* Hold on. If you just thought that to yourself, then you have missed the whole point. You don't have *to become* righteous; if you are born again, *you are righteous.* Therefore, if the fruit of prayer is not showing up in your life, you need to begin to acknowledge that you are righteous.

Say it right now! Say, "I am the righteousness of God in Christ Jesus." Say it out loud so that God can hear it, the devil can hear it and you can hear it. I'm telling you that when it dawns on you that you are righteous, that's when you will live free from sin and its effects. That's when you will pray with power.

If you know who you are in Christ, then you will know that when you pray God hears you and the army of heaven is behind you. You will know that things are moving and shaking because you prayed. Righteousness makes you bold.

2. A revelation of righteousness will empower you to rule and reign as royalty in this life.

Look at what Romans 5 tells us.

> **Romans 5:17 (AMP)**
> For if because of one man's trespass (lapse, offense) death reigned through that one, much more surely will those who receive [God's] overflowing grace (unmerited favor) and the free gift of righteousness [putting them into right standing with Himself] reign as kings in life through the one man Jesus Christ (the Messiah, the Anointed One).

There should be no sin big enough to dominate you as you reign as a king in this life through Jesus Christ. Kings don't let anything push them around, and you shouldn't either. Kings have everything they want; they do whatever they want whenever they want to do it.

When kings say, "Jump!" people say, "How high?" Make no mistake—whether you are male or female—Jesus told you to reign. Are you ruling over temptation? Pull out your scepter and reign over sin in your life. Jesus gave you dominion.

3. A revelation of righteousness will help you grow up and eat the meat of God's Word.

Look at what Hebrews tell us.

> **Hebrews 5:13-14 (NKJV)**
> 13 For everyone who partakes only of milk is unskilled in the word of righteousness, for he is a babe.
> 14 But solid food belongs to those who are of full age, that is, those who by reason of use have their senses exercised to discern both good and evil.

Are you ready to move up out of the spiritual nursery and get off the milk bottle? We all start out as babies both in the natural realm and the spiritual realm. But when little Johnny turns 16, it's troubling when he wants a milk bottle or still wants his steak cut into little pieces. When we grow past milk and begin eating the meat of God's Word, we're better able to say no to temptation and sin.

Consequently, baby Christians who are not willing to get off the spiritual bottle and move on to the meat of the Word don't have a grasp of their righteousness, and sin is likely to dominate them.

4. You will be strong and courageous.

Individuals who don't have a revelation of their righteousness will walk in sin consciousness. What's the solution? Isaiah 41 shows us below.

> **Isaiah 41:10**
> Fear thou not; for I am with thee: be not dismayed; for I am thy God: I will strengthen thee; yea, I will help thee; yea, I

will uphold thee with the right hand of my righteousness.

God says that He's upholding you with the right hand of His righteousness, and all you have to do is accept what Jesus has already done for you. You cannot earn it. You cannot buy it. But you can have it. It's a free gift.

Don't let sin or fear creep into your life in any way, shape or form. Jesus wasn't afraid of anything, and you don't have to be either. Jesus commanded the winds and the waves to stop. When people ran out of food, He multiplied it. "Oh, but, Mark, that's Jesus," someone might say. Yes, but when you speak His Words, you also can declare that circumstances and situations change. God said He would uphold you with His righteousness, so be bold.

5. With a revelation of your righteousness, you will refuse to be a slave of sin.

Nothing good comes from sin. It may bring pleasure for a short while, but it quickly turns into an ugly picture with a dead end. Look what the apostle Paul says in the passage below.

> **Romans 6:16-23 (AMP)**
> 16 Do you not know that if you continually surrender yourselves to anyone to do his will, you are the slaves of him whom you obey, whether that be to sin, which leads to death, or to obedience which leads to righteousness (right doing and right standing with God)?
>
> 17 But thank God, though you were once slaves of sin, you have become obedient with all your heart to the standard of teaching in which you were instructed and to which you were committed.

> 18 And having been set free from sin, you have become the servants of righteousness (of conformity to the divine will in thought, purpose, and action).
>
> 19 I am speaking in familiar human terms because of your natural limitations. For as you yielded your bodily members [and faculties] as servants to impurity and ever increasing lawlessness, so now yield your bodily members [and faculties] once for all as servants to righteousness (right being and doing) [which leads] to sanctification.
>
> 20 For when you were slaves of sin, you were free in regard to righteousness.
>
> 21 But then what benefit (return) did you get from the things of which you are now ashamed? [None] for the end of those things is death.
>
> 22 But now since you have been set free from sin and have become the slaves of God, you have your present reward in holiness and its end is eternal life.
>
> 23 For the wages which sin pays is death, but the [bountiful] free gift of God is eternal life through (in union with) Jesus Christ our Lord.

When you get a hold of the fact that you're no slave to sin, you'll never again say things like: *I cannot control myself. I got into trouble because I'm sort of wishy-washy. I cannot quit. I can't get over this or that. It's just my personality. I can't help myself.* Oh, yes you can! You have been set free, so walk free. Walk in righteousness.

6. If you have a revelation of righteousness, you will receive correction and be better for it.

Good parents correct their children, and God is no different. If you are God's child, He will correct you. If you receive that correction and adjust your life accordingly, you'll walk in righteousness. What you cannot afford to do is pretend like God is not dealing with you and keep on doing things that are wrong. In that case, the righteousness that legally belongs to you will not work in your life, and sin will continue to dominate you. Look at the instruction Hebrews 12 offers us:

> **Hebrews 12:11**
> Now no chastening for the present seemeth to be joyous, but grievous: nevertheless afterward it yieldeth the peaceable fruit of righteousness unto them which are exercised thereby.

God corrects us because He loves us. He doesn't set out to punish us, but when we do wrong He doesn't wink and say, "Oh well! Those stupid humans will never get it." No, He trains us and disciplines us as any good parent on earth would do. As every human parent will testify, bad behavior that goes undisciplined will cause great trouble for our children later.

The Amplified Bible translates verse 11 this way:

> **Hebrews 12:11**
> For the time being no discipline brings joy, but seems grievous and painful; but afterwards it yields a peaceable fruit of righteousness to those who have been trained by it [a harvest of fruit which consists in righteousness—in conformity to God's will in purpose, thought, and action, resulting in right living and right standing with God].

I want to make sure you understand that God does discipline, teach and trains us with His Word and by His Spirit. But God does not send sickness, disease, calamities and disasters to correct or teach His children. John 10:10 said Jesus came to give us abundant life, and it's the devil who steals, kills and destroys. James 1:17 says every good and perfect gift came down from the Father above.

For example, God has corrected you as you've read this book. Every time you've thought, "Ouch. Yeah, that's me. That's true. I'm guilty," that was the Word correcting you. Every time you've known in your heart, "Oh yeah, I need to change that area of my life," that was the Holy Spirit convicting you and prompting you. Sometimes it is painful, but if you will make the adjustments you'll save yourself a whole lot of trouble, and you'll gain the "peaceable fruit of righteousness."

Even now, you stand at a fork in the road. Will you break way from sin and follow righteousness? You choose. Which way are you going? The choice to walk in righteousness is yours alone, but once you make that choice, all of heaven will help you walk it out. You and I could never overcome sin on our own; we must have the help of the Holy Spirit. He teaches us, trains us and coaches us through life.

Let's look at Romans 6 in The Amplified Bible that explains more about how righteousness sets us free from the acts of sin.

> **Romans 6:17-18**
> 17 But thank God, though you were once slaves of sin, you have become obedient with all your heart to the standard of teaching in which you were instructed and to which you were committed.
>
> 18 And having been set free from sin, you have become the *servants of righteousness* (of conformity to the divine will in thought, purpose, and action).

"Where do I sign up to become a servant of righteousness?" someone might ask. You obey the teachings of God's Word. You conform to

God's thoughts, which are higher than your thoughts. You line up with God's purposes and actions or God's ways, which are higher than your ways. And, again, you receive the help of the Holy Spirit.

Trust me, we cannot overcome temptation and sin by willpower; it's done by God-power. If we rely on willpower, we will weaken and fail. But when we allow God's power to work in our lives, we will be set free from sin and the desire to sin. Of course, we will still have the flesh to deal with and the devil will still try to entice us with the lusts of the flesh, but we will no longer be a slave to sin. Empowered and changed by the righteousness of God in Christ, we will no longer yield our bodies to its desires; we will be a slave to righteousness.

Romans 6:22 in The Amplified Bible says, "But now since you have been set free from sin and have become the slaves of God, you have your present reward in holiness and its end is eternal life." Praise God, you have the reward of holiness and its paycheck of eternal life with God in heaven. But the reward of holiness is much more. It's also living free from the bondages of sin here and now.

Let me encourage you to meditate on these three verses to lodge the truth of righteousness deep in your heart: 2 Corinthians 5:17-21, 1 Corinthians 1:30-31 and Romans 10:1-10.

The more you grasp a revelation of righteousness, the better off you'll be. Maybe you've felt that up until now your Christian walk has been the right walk, but a hard walk. Let me encourage you that righteousness will make hard things easy. If you'll position yourself to rule and reign through the righteousness Jesus has given you, you'll no longer struggle with sin, sickness, poverty or any work of the devil. Righteousness is how you're able to walk in the position ordained for you as a son and a daughter of the Most High God.

CHAPTER 8
THE MIND IS A TERRIBLE THING TO WASTE

Your mind is powerful. It can nip sin in the bud or set the stage for temptation to run rampant and drive you to destruction. In fact, your mind is a battlefield and it's where you fight your biggest battles. Whatever you set your mind on is eventually what happens in your life.

After all, a person doesn't just go to Wal-Mart one day and fall into adultery as we said early on. A person doesn't just drive the kids to school one morning and suddenly decide to rob a bank on the way home. That's not how it happens. That's not the process of sin. Sin starts in the mind; it all begins with a single thought and it builds from there. Sin and lust are conceived in the mind.

That's why the Bible tells us that if we will train our mind not to think things we shouldn't think, we can close the door on sin before it even starts. In fact, the Bible is pretty clear about that the fact that if we keep our minds focused on God's Word, victory and success can be ours.

Joshua 1:8 says, "This Book of the Law shall not depart from your mouth, but you shall meditate in it day and night, that you may observe to do according to all that is written in it. For then you will make your way prosperous, and then you will have good success" (NKJV). If you keep your mind focused on God's Word, you'll walk in prosperity, health and wisdom and fulfill what God has called you to do.

God is not trying to spoil your good times. God wants you to be free from sin, and He wants you to be the best you can be. He wants your family to be the freest, happiest, wisest, richest family in town, and that's why God instructs you to think a whole new way.

SAVING YOUR SOUL

We talked earlier about how we receive a new nature when we are born again; our spirit or inner person of the heart becomes new. Our spirit isn't fixed up a little; we receive a completely new nature. But our minds remain the same as they were before we became born again and need to be retrained according to God's Word.

Let's look at it this way. Maybe you have heard it said that your mind is like a computer, and it's true. But in the case of becoming born again, nothing happens to your mental computer. No reset button is pushed; no new program is downloaded or installed. Practically speaking, you are in desperate need of new software and technical assistance. Your mind needs to be filled with new information and a new way of thinking. You need to think like God thinks and that process of adjusting what and how you think is what the Bible calls *renewing your mind*.

This is where I feel a lot of people miss it and remain stuck in a life of sin. People get born again, even filled with the Holy Spirit, but they don't do anything with their soul—or their mind, will and emotions—so they still live, think and talk like they did before.

The word *soul* is sometimes hard for people to understand because of the terms we use in Christian circles. For instance, people will say, "Wow—we had 10 souls saved." But what they really mean is that 10 people were born again or 10 people made a commitment to receive Jesus as their Lord and Savior. As we mentioned in earlier chapters, each of us is a three-part being: spirit, soul and body. So when the 10 people were born again, they received a new divine nature in their spirits. Their bodies still need to be disciplined and controlled, and their souls—or mind, will and emotions—still need to be retrained.

As a pastor I've often seen the anointing of God deliver people in our church services from drugs, pornography, alcohol, gambling, stealing, lying, cheating or whatever habit troubled them. Yet, most people don't realize that in order to continue walking in victory, they still will need to renew their minds. Only then can they be free of the problem for life.

Without a doubt, the anointing can remove the addiction, but addictions are not only physical; they are also mental.

So until a person gets his or her mind renewed, the sin problem won't be fixed.

You see, before we were born again, we thought like the world, acted like the world and followed in the footsteps of our father the devil. We saw earlier in Ephesians 2:3 that sin dogged our tracks because we were "...obeying the impulses of the flesh and the thoughts of the mind [our cravings dictated by our senses and our dark imaginings]. We were then by nature children of [God's] wrath and heirs of [His] indignation, like the rest of mankind" (AMP).

In simple terms, your mind was a mess before you were born again. It was programmed by this world. The Bible says it was influenced by the devil, who is the god of this world system. We didn't think right and couldn't help it because we were influenced by the devil himself.

You might be thinking, *Well, I'm telling you right now that my mind was not controlled by the devil.* But the truth is that before you were born again, your mind wasn't governed by God and His Word either. You had nothing to combat those evil tendencies, and therefore you could not help but yield your thoughts to the god of this world (2 Corinthians 4:4). It's important to understand the tremendous influence the enemy had over your mind before you were born again, so you'll understand the great importance of renewing your mind after you're born again.

Romans 8:5 says, "For those who are according to the flesh and are controlled by its unholy desires set their minds on and pursue those things which gratify the flesh. ..." Before we were born again, all we could do was follow after our flesh because our nature had not been changed. We were of this world with our minds set on how to gratify our flesh. We thought about sin, got a picture of sin in our minds and then set out to satisfy our flesh. Whatever it craved, we said yes because our mind was set to sin.

Then look at surrounding verses in Romans 8.

> **Romans 8:4-8 (AMP)**
> 4 So that the righteous and just requirement of the Law might be fully met in us who live and move not in the ways of the flesh but in the ways of the Spirit [our lives governed not by the standards and according to the dictates of the flesh, but controlled by the Holy Spirit].
>
> 5 For those who are according to the flesh and are controlled by its unholy desires set their minds on and pursue those things which gratify the flesh, but those who are according to the Spirit and are controlled by the desires of the Spirit set their minds

> on and seek those things which gratify the [Holy] Spirit.
>
> 6 Now the mind of the flesh [which is sense and reason without the Holy Spirit] is death [death that comprises all the miseries arising from sin, both here and hereafter]. But the mind of the [Holy] Spirit is life and [soul] peace [both now and forever].
>
> 7 [That is] because the mind of the flesh [with its carnal thoughts and purposes] is hostile to God, for it does not submit itself to God's Law; indeed it cannot.
>
> 8 So then those who are living the life of the flesh [catering to the appetites and impulses of their carnal nature] cannot please or satisfy God, or be acceptable to Him.

Here's the battle. Your mind wants to set its sights on what feels good to the flesh, and it doesn't plan to let anything get in its way. That's why your mind has to be taught to think differently. If you don't retrain and renew your mind, then you're in for a real knock-down drag-out with the devil. That's why a lot of Christians who love God are still sinning even though they really don't want to sin.

Face facts. Knowing something is wrong and doing something about it are two totally different things. So I'm telling you that if you want to do something about sin, you must reprogram your mind. In fact, Romans 8 makes the choice clear. Either you will refocus your mind on God's Word and pleasing God, or you will keep your mind set on the things of this world and how to gratify the cravings of the flesh at every turn.

Verse 6 lays out what happens if you make the wrong choice. It says, "Now the mind of the flesh [which is sense and reason without the Holy Spirit] is death." Our mind left to think its own way—without the Holy Spirit—results in death. Why? Because without the Word of

God and the Spirit of God, the human mind produces sin, and sin always produces a paycheck of death.

"Well, I'm still alive, Pastor Mark, and I've sinned plenty," someone might say. I'm glad you're still alive; it gives you more time to choose to walk in the goodness of God. But look back at the point where you got off in sin, and I'm sure you'll find that it produced death in a situation. Did it produce death or an end to a relationship, a business, a ministry? Sin is sometimes fun for a season, but the season always comes to an end. Aren't you glad for the mercy of God?

Notice the rest of verse 6, "Now the mind of the flesh [which is sense and reason without the Holy Spirit] is death [death that comprises all the miseries arising from sin, both here and hereafter]. But the mind of the [Holy] Spirit is life and [soul] peace." How many of you want some soul peace?

Verse 7 goes on to say that the mind of the flesh with its carnal thoughts and purposes is hostile to God. An unrenewed mind is hostile to God, and that's not a good place to be.

Like a lot of people, I heard the stories of the Bible as a little boy, but I didn't have much practical teaching from God's Word. By age 12 I got born again and loved God, but soon got off into sin. I still loved God and respected Him, but I didn't serve Him. Frankly, at that time I didn't understand a lot of what I read in the Bible.

By my early 20s, I was a very liberal thinker. Most things that I oppose today I embraced when I was in my early 20s. Why? Because even though I was born again at the age of 12, my mind was still contrary to the Word of God. I had heard little of God's Word and understood even less. My mind couldn't think like God because I didn't know and understand what God thought. I didn't retrain my mind to think the way God thinks.

It's the same with a lot of people. They might love God, but they never develop the space between their ears. Yet, what's done or not done with the mind determines whether or not we will be successful in our walk with God. We have to choose to renew the mind because left alone it will oppose God. Verse 8 said "…those who are living a life of the flesh … cannot please or satisfy God, or be acceptable to him." Make no mistake. These words were written to Christians in the early church; they were not written to sinners. These words also are written for today's Church—for you and me.

Sure, it would be easy if all we had to do was call church folks down to the front in a service and pray for all sin to disappear. That would be a great quick-fix-microwave-drive-thru sort of experience. But everything is not always microwave and drive-thru with God. God is a good God and He wants to help us, but we also have to do our part. In fact, there are many things that God has for us that we will never receive unless we do our part. God is always doing His part 100 percent, and His side is always good. But there's a God side and a man side to receiving from God, and so what you do on your end matters.

As a pastor I sometimes see Christians who got born again decades before, but they failed to begin renewing their minds. Unfortunately, those are the Christians who either fall right back into sin or wrestle and struggle with sin their entire lives.

The whole point is this. You may have gotten born again, but your mind did not. So unless you retrain your mind it will think like it always thought. It will still think the same ugly, impure, lustful, mean, unkind, unholy thoughts it always thought and produce the same ugly, impure, lustful, mean, unkind, unholy desires it always produced before you were born again. Actually, is it any wonder why people have such a problem with sin? The good news is that you *can* renew your mind. You can do this because God said you can.

Just by living in this world we're continually faced with things that try to entice and tease the lust of our flesh. So if we want to live in victory—and you do or you wouldn't be reading this book—then you must renew your mind. If you're going to break free, stay free and live free of sin, you've got to think differently than you have before.

HOW TO RENEW YOUR MIND

Let's turn to God's Word to learn more about *how* we can renew our minds and think differently. Writing to the Christians in Rome—and teaching us today—the apostle Paul lays out a key scripture on this topic.

Romans 12:2 says, "...Do not be conformed to this world, but be transformed by the renewing of your mind, that you may prove what *is* that good and acceptable and perfect will of God" (NKJV). The word *transform* in the Greek means a metamorphosis, and that's exactly what our minds need. We need to transform our minds in the same way that a caterpillar transforms into a butterfly. It's a radical change! The process of going from a caterpillar to a butterfly creates something altogether renewed.

When you think about it, caterpillars aren't all that good looking, but butterflies are beautiful. I believe Paul is telling us that it's time for us to turn into something beautiful. God wants to take this thing called the mind—that pushes us into sin, makes us do things that are dark and ugly—and transform it into something of beauty.

Psalm 23:3 says, "He restores my soul" (NKJV). We hear that word *restore* a lot of times when people talk about restoring cars or antique furniture. It means to bring an object back to its original state of beauty. Is it automatic? No. Restoration takes a lot of hard work, but eventually the original beauty shines through.

James tells us how to begin the restoration process on our minds in James 1:21, which says, "...Lay aside all filthiness and overflow of wickedness, and receive with meekness the implanted word, which is able to save your souls" (NKJV). James is explaining that the key to renewing our minds is to receive God's Word with a meek or teachable spirit.

As you give the Word first place in your life, meditate on the Word, think about the Word and act on the Word, it begins to transform your life. Your thoughts will change your words, and your words will change your actions. This is where the rubber meets the road. So many people love God, but they don't find the pathway to victory because of this one thing. It's not enough to love God; we must obey God. If we obey God, then victory is ours.

I cannot count the number of people who have been in my office over the years in tears saying, "I don't understand how I fell into sin. I love God." I don't question their love, and I'm sure God doesn't either, but it takes more than loving God to walk in victory. We have to obey His Word.

THE BATTLEFIELD OF THE MIND

You're at war—whether you realize it or not—and the battlefield is right between your ears. It's a battle to walk in light or darkness. It is a battle to obey or disobey God. It's literally a battle between good and evil, and you decide the winner.

If you haven't figured it out already, you cannot afford to think like you did before, and here's why: If you continue to think like you did before you were saved, then you will act like you did before you were saved. Actually, one of the biggest triggers causing you to sin is the thought patterns you developed while you were living and practicing sin.

Born-again folks who do not renew their minds are at a tremendous disadvantage. The enemy continually attacks and performs sabotage missions from inside their own heads. It's unfair, but it's true. No wonder people are frustrated and defeated and still living in sin. What is the answer? A great transformation must take place, and we must use our God-given weapons to defeat the enemy.

Let's look at a key scripture that will point the way to victory.

> **2 Corinthians 10:4-5**
>
> 4 (For the weapons of our warfare are not carnal, but mighty through God to the pulling down of strong holds;)
>
> 5 Casting down imaginations, and every high thing that exalteth itself against the knowledge of God, and bringing into captivity every thought to the obedience of Christ.

Did you notice the word *stronghold*? It refers to a fortified place, where people in days gone by would build forts high on a hill to be protected from enemy attack. Unfortunately, however, the devil oftentimes builds strongholds in our minds. He builds up fortified places or patterns of thinking that can destroy us.

These strongholds or patterns of thinking are imaginations, thoughts, arguments and reasonings that try to challenge the knowledge of God. These strongholds are any thought pattern in your mind that opposes the Word of God and keeps you from walking in God's highest and best. Whether we call them strongholds or not, we all have thoughts like these.

Someone might say, "Maybe just people with alcoholism or drug problems or pornography or some huge problems have strongholds like these." No, we all have thoughts and strongholds in our minds that oppose the will and purpose of God in our lives. And we all need to get rid of them.

In a book called *Dressed to Kill,* author Rick Renner shares this about strongholds.

> Individuals who have these kinds of strongholds in their lives are in bondage both *mentally* and *emotionally.* Sometime in the past the enemy located an open door

in their lives. Then after passing through that entrance into their minds, he began the process of taking their thoughts captive through his lies. The result is always the same: Strongholds are built that act as a prison, preventing these individuals from breaking free to fulfill their God-ordained purpose on this earth.

How serious is this? It's serious. If believers never do anything about renewing their minds, these strongholds will prevent them from obeying and fulfilling their God-ordained purpose.

If we don't learn to take captive thoughts that oppose God's Word, then one day these negative thoughts will take us captive. We must arrest these thoughts and take them prisoner before they lock shackles on our hands and feet and keep us bound to sin for life. Armed with the Word of God, we are to cast down every high thing that exalts itself against the knowledge of God and bring into captivity every thought—*every single thought*—to the obedience of Christ.

Notice how The Amplified Bible translates Paul's instruction to us.

> **2 Corinthians 10:4-5 (AMP)**
> 4 For the weapons of our warfare are not physical [weapons of flesh and blood], but they are mighty before God for the overthrow and destruction of strongholds,
>
> 5 [Inasmuch as we] refute arguments and theories and reasonings and every proud and lofty thing that sets itself up against the [true] knowledge of God; and we lead every thought and purpose away captive into the obedience of Christ (the Messiah, the Anointed One).

Paul tells us to overthrow and destroy strongholds by refusing to think a thought that opposes God's Word. Whatever God says and declares about a thing is what we should say and declare about a thing. In fact, I know this will come as a big surprise to some people, but you don't have to receive and meditate on every thought that pops into your head.

Refuse it! Don't take it!

Every thought that comes into your head isn't yours anyway. The devil pesters you with thoughts of all kinds—about sin, sickness, poverty and death. For example, maybe you have something physically wrong in your body and the devil plants the thought, "You're probably going to die." Have you ever had the thought, "What if I can't pay my bills and I go broke?" Do you know what the devil is trying to do? He's trying to plant that thought in your mind so you'll begin to think that way and talk that way. That's called a stronghold and strongholds produce results.

But God has given you authority over your life and what happens to you. God has given you thousands of Bible promises, and He expects you to use your faith to obtain them. On the other hand, the devil wants you to agree with him so he can ruin your life.

"How do you know if a thought is from God or the devil and which is which?" someone might ask. God's thoughts are written down in the Bible from Genesis 1 to Revelation 22. So every one of God's thoughts that you need in order to walk in victory is in His Word for you to read. So no more garbage in, garbage out when it comes to your mind. As we put in God's Word, it will remove the garbage. As we make God's thoughts our thoughts, we'll find ourselves on the road to victory.

If a thought goes against God's Word, it's from the devil. If it steals, kills or destroys, it's from the devil. Those are thoughts to cast down. If a thought doesn't agree with God's Word, kick it out of your mind. Take those thoughts captive. Arrest them. Take them prisoner. Armed with the weapon of the Word, tell that thought, "You're not allowed. Surrender. You're out." Then replace those negative thoughts with the truth of God's Word.

Maybe you think, *I'm a failure and a loser.* Maybe you think, *I'll never amount to anything.* Maybe you're married, but you cannot stop thinking about that guy or gal at work. Maybe you're overcome with thoughts of pornography or addictive substances. Do these thoughts oppose God's Word? Yes, no question about it. Then take them captive. Arrest them. Toss them out. Refuse to think them, and replace them with what God says.

You can't just let those thoughts go crazy and run wild in your mind because if you do, they'll eventually become strongholds. Thoughts will make pictures and begin to create reality. When I say *dog*, you get a mental picture of a dog. When I say cat, you get a picture of a cat. When I say *a million dollars*, you get a picture of green cash. These pictures build images and imaginations. It's the same with wrong thoughts, and you can't afford to let negative ones hang around.

So what do you do when negative thoughts come to mind? Talk to them. When I was on an airplane going to India, and the plane began bouncing around, the devil shot plenty of thoughts my way: "*You're going to die. The plane is going down.*" Did I give in to those fearful thoughts? Did I start imagining my funeral and wondering what it would be like? Did I begin to cry? Did I say goodbye to loved ones? No. I opened my mouth and said, "With long life God will satisfy me and show me His salvation" (Psalm 91:16). "I will live and not die and proclaim the works of the Lord" (Psalm 118:17). In other words, when the devil fired shots at me, I fired back with the truth of God's Word.

That's how you take thoughts captive. Your mouth speaking the Word takes a thought captive while you're speaking and releases faith to cleanse your mind. That's also how you can arrest thoughts of sin and temptation that come across your mind. Listen to me. You must take this step to control thoughts of temptation or, before you know it, you'll be sitting in a pastor's office with your head in your hands saying, "Oh, my God, how did this sin happen?"

Begin meditating on what God has to say about your situation. For example, if you have a thought of worry, begin to meditate on scriptures such as 1 Peter 5:7, which say, "Casting all your care upon Him, for He cares for you" (NKJV). Begin to say from your heart and mouth, "I refuse to worry because my God cares for me. He has taken care of my cares. I am carefree."

If you have thoughts about anger issues, confess scriptures on the love of God. If you have trouble with any area of sin, begin to confess scriptures on being in Him or in Jesus Christ. After all, it's hard to be conscious of being in oneness with Jesus Christ and be conscious of sin at the same time. As we confess our union with Jesus Christ, sin has to drop off.

Let me give you a tool that's worked for me many times. In fact, try this with me now. Begin to count to 10 in your mind. Then when I say, *"praise the Lord,"* you say it aloud immediately.

OK, begin counting in your mind. Now say out loud, *"Praise the Lord!"*

What happened to your counting when you spoke, *"Praise the Lord!"* out loud? Did the counting stop? Yes, of course! Your brain had to unhook from the counting because it had to instruct and connect with your vocal chords to speak. Likewise, even though the devil may pester you with thoughts, if you'll speak God's Word out loud, your brain will unhook from the worries or temptations and quote the Word.

This is a tried-and-true plan to short circuit negative thoughts. Just open your mouth and say what the Word says about your situation to combat sin. Get serious about thoughts that pester you. Don't let one of them go unchecked. Listen, it's a serious thing to control your thoughts because left untreated negative thoughts spread like cancer and destroy everything in their path.

"How long do I have to resist thoughts of sin and temptation? I've got consistent thoughts that drive me nuts." As long as it takes. You've got to be stronger than the enemy. You've got to demonstrate more perseverance than the devil does because he's a defeated foe. Best yet, if you continue to resist him, what does the Bible say will happen? James 4:7 says, "...resist the devil, and he will flee." The word *flee* in the dictionary means to run in terror, and that means with God's Word you'll put the devil on the run.

The one thing you cannot do is ignore negative thoughts. If you do, they can really put you in bondage. Worries can fly at you so fast and furious that you end up in a tailspin of panic. You also cannot pray away thoughts nor can someone else pray them away for you. No, the solution is that you arrest rogue thoughts and take them prisoner. Replace them with God's Word.

The only way we can successfully change our thinking is to renew our minds. We transform our minds by taking every thought contrary to God's Word captive. We need to cast down every thought and every imagination or mental picture that does not line up with God's Word and replace it with the truth of God's Word.

GIVE YOUR MIND A BATH

God's Word will give our mind a bath. Ephesians 5:26 says, "...sanctify and cleanse ... with the washing of water by the word." The background of this scripture talks about washing the church with the Word because the Word is a cleansing agent when applied to whatever needs cleaning.

John 17:17 says, "Sanctify them by your truth. Your word is truth" (NKJV). John 15:3 says, "Now ye are clean through the word which I have spoken unto you." You and I must let the truth cleanse our mind, and God's Word is the only thing that can do it.

We must allow God's Word to sanctify us or set us apart from the lusts of the flesh. When we continuously live a life that is sanctified; we won't yield to what our flesh wants. God gives us the ability to take His Word and use it like a washcloth with soap and water to scrub our minds clean from sin.

Another scripture that talks about the mind is found in Hebrews 12:3, which says, "…consider him [Jesus] that endured such contradiction [hostility] … lest ye be wearied and *faint in your minds.*" Did you realize that you can become weary and faint in your mind? The devil will try to wear you out to the point that you faint mentally.

Two different times in my life I've fainted physically, and it's like you suddenly just lose all power. You can imagine that the devil would have a heyday if he could get you to a place where you lost all power and control mentally. Sin would be knocking at your door. But did you notice that this scripture also shows you how *not* to faint? It says those who faint get weary because they fail to consider Jesus or keep their minds focused on the way of escape He provides for us. That means if you keep your mind on Jesus, you won't get weary and faint.

Isaiah 26:3 goes further and says, God will "…keep him in perfect peace, Whose mind is stayed on You [God], Because he trusts in You [God]" (NKJV). The New Living Translation says, "You will keep in perfect peace all who trust in you, all whose thoughts are fixed on you!" That's your solution. Keep your mind stayed on Jesus. Keep your thoughts fixed on Him, and He will keep you in perfect peace. Perfect peace has nothing in common with sin.

Another step in renewing your mind is to accept the promises of God concerning your mind. How do you accept a Bible promise? You hear it, believe it and release it. Look at these two scriptures. Romans 10:17 says that faith comes by hearing the Word of God, and one of the best ways to hear the Word is to hear it coming out your own mouth. Then notice what the Bible says in Mark 11:23, "…whoever says to this mountain, 'Be removed and be cast into the sea,' and does not doubt in his heart, but believes that those things he says will be done, he will have whatever he says" (NKJV).

So when thoughts fly against your mind that don't line up with God's Word, open your Bible and find out what God says about the situation. Then speak those words aloud and let them renew and retrain your mind.

Here are several verses where God has spoken about your mind to help you:

• First Corinthians 2:16 says, "…We have the mind of Christ." Boldly begin to say, "Because Jesus lives in me, I have the mind of Christ. I think His thoughts, which are found in His Word."

• Philippians 2:5 says, "Let this mind be in you which was also in Christ Jesus." Begin to say aloud, "I have the same mind-set as Christ Jesus." Even if your current thoughts don't even remotely seem like thoughts that Jesus would think, say this verse anyway and watch what happens. You will begin to measure and weigh your thoughts, and the Holy Spirit will challenge thoughts you have that don't line up with God's Word.

• Philippians 4 says you can keep yourself from thinking wrong thoughts because the Bible says you can. In fact, the Bible even tells you what to think on.

> **Philippians 4:8 (NKJV)**
> Finally, brethren, whatever things are true, whatever things are noble, whatever things are just, whatever things are pure, whatever things are lovely, whatever things are of good report, if there is any virtue and if there is anything praiseworthy—meditate on these things.

Here's the ultimate God-ordained Bible test for thoughts. In Philippians 4:8 the Holy Spirit spelled out exactly what we should and should not think about. So if a thought doesn't meet the Philippians 4:8 test, kick it out and refuse to think it. Think God's way and you'll find yourself no longer shackled to sin.

CHAPTER 9
A MULTIPLAN ATTACK ON SIN

We've talked about many "how-to" keys that will enable us to break free and stay free of sin, but we're not done yet. After all, the more supernatural tools we learn how to operate, the more empowered and equipped we'll be to walk in the freedom that God has provided for us. The Bible doesn't list only one key to our freedom because there's not just one single thing to know or to do; there's not simply one switch we flip to eliminate sin in our lives.

Walking with God is just that—a walk—and there are a number of things we need to know. If there were only one or two things we needed to know, I guess God would have given us just one book in the Bible, two at the most. But did you notice there are 66? I also know that God doesn't waste words, so there are different keys for different people at different times in their lives. Which one do you need to know? All of them. So let's consider a multiplan attack on sin.

THE ANOINTING

One of the most important supernatural helps available is what the Bible calls the anointing or the manifest presence of God. This manifest power of God can be sensed in the spirit or the inward person of the heart, but it also can be tangible. Whether you sense the anointing inwardly or outwardly, it's the power of God that delivers His promises of freedom into your life.

Jesus boldly proclaimed the anointing was upon Him to preach the gospel, deliver the captives and heal the broken hearted. Notice the words of Luke 4.

> **Luke 4:18-19**
> 18 The Spirit of the Lord is upon me, because he hath anointed me to preach the gospel to the poor; he hath sent me to heal the brokenhearted, to preach deliverance to the captives, and recovering of sight to the blind, to set at liberty them that are bruised,
> 19 To preach the acceptable year of the Lord.

It says that Jesus came to set at liberty those that were bruised, but what does *bruised* mean? It means to have a sore spot left over from an injury. I'm sure you've noticed that the devil likes to poke at sore spots in your life, and it hurts when he does. He pokes at places that are bruised because you have consistently yielded to the lusts of your flesh, and it's caused trouble. But the good news is the anointing liberates those who are bruised or hurt by sin.

Let me encourage you to come in contact with the power of God as often as possible. Get into services where the presence of God is manifested or worship God at home until His presence fills the room. If you want emancipation from the bondage of sin, you must yield to God's power and anointing.

Second Corinthians 3:17 says, "Now the Lord is that Spirit, and where the Spirit of the Lord is, there is liberty (emancipation from bondage, freedom)" (AMP). When you allow the anointing or the presence of God to invade your life and come into contact with your flesh, freedom is all yours.

This anointing we're talking about always destroys bondage. Isaiah 10:27 says, the "yoke shall be destroyed because of the anointing." That means the sinful junk we're dealing with can be destroyed by coming in contact with the power of God.

But the anointing of God and the power of God are not stand-alone solutions. We need to keep ourselves in the Word of God and continually seek the presence of God. If we want to walk in victory over sin, then we need to attend churches that pursue the presence of God not only in theory, but also in practice. The anointing has changed my life, and I know it will change yours.

The anointing comes to destroy the bondage that's held you in sin. Isaiah 42:7 says, "To open the blind eyes, to bring out the prisoners from prison, and them that sit in darkness out of the prison house." The anointing breaks off your shackles and leaves them in the prison house of sin and you walk out free.

Make no mistake that Jesus broke the power of bondage in your life when He was on the cross some 2,000 years ago. The door to the prison house is unlocked and standing wide open. All that's left for you to do is believe it's God's will for you to be free and walk in the freedom.

Regular doses of the power of God will help to keep your flesh in check. Other than the physical act of dying, there's no way to completely get rid of the lust of your flesh, but the manifest presence of God goes a long way toward equipping you to resist the devil. We need the anointing, and that is why it is available.

Acts 2:17 says, "And it shall come to pass in the last days, saith God I will pour out of my spirit upon all flesh...." In this instance, the scripture is talking about the Holy Spirit being poured out on all mankind. But I believe this scripture also helps us understand how the Holy Spirit can help us keep our flesh under.

You see, God's Spirit is not only within you as a born-again believer, the Holy Spirit can also come on you. For example, on the day of Pentecost, the Bible said the Spirit of God came on each one of the people in the Upper Room as cloven tongues of fire. The fire of God forever changed the 120 people that day.

Prior to the day of Pentecost, Peter had denied Jesus three times. Yet, the fire changed him so much on that day that he was bold enough to stand up and preach to everyone who would hear him. The fire of God caused Peter's flesh to go from hiding in the Upper Room to proclaiming the gospel message on the streets of Jerusalem. The fire or the power of God on your flesh will change you so thoroughly that you will act differently as well.

Malachi 3:2-3 talks about how Jesus will come like a refiner's fire and fuller's soap and clean you up. After you are born again, you are clean on the inside, but your flesh that's inclined to sin still needs work. So thank God for the fire of God that can bring change to us.

I've watched many people come to church and get on fire for God, but then slowly drift away and eventually return to a sinful life. One reason they slid back into sin is that they left the fire. They thought they could conquer sin on their own, but they were wrong. If we could handle sin on our own, we wouldn't need God. We will never get to a place where we do not need God's power.

Will one dose of the power be enough to set you free from sin? Maybe. But you'll need regular doses to stay free. Get in the manifest presence of God as often as you can because again 2 Corinthians 3:17

says, "…Where the Spirit of the Lord is, there is liberty (emancipation from bondage, freedom)" (AMP). Let me encourage you to get in a church where God's Word is taught and God is allowed to move, where the Holy Spirit is allowed to manifest and given free course. Regularly position yourself in meetings where people know how to worship God and the power of God is in demonstration. It will forever change you from the inside out.

In fact, notice how Paul teaches in the following scriptures about how the power of God works from the inside out in our lives.

> **Romans 8:8-13 (NKJV)**
> 8 So then, those who are in the flesh cannot please God.
>
> 9 But you are not in the flesh but in the Spirit, if indeed the Spirit of God dwells in you. Now if anyone does not have the Spirit of Christ, he is not His.
>
> 10 And if Christ is in you, the body is dead because of sin, but the Spirit is life because of righteousness.
>
> **11 But if the Spirit of Him who raised Jesus from the dead dwells in you, He who raised Christ from the dead will also give life to your mortal bodies through His Spirit who dwells in you.**
>
> 12 Therefore, brethren, we are debtors—not to the flesh, to live according to the flesh.
>
> 13 For if you live according to the flesh you will die; but if by the Spirit you put to death the deeds of the body, you will live.

Let's concentrate on verse 11, which tells us something many people seem to miss. I've heard many Bible teachers share on this familiar scripture verse about how the power of God quickens our mortal bodies to heal us. It's true, and thank God for it. But did you realize that in this setting Paul is actually talking about living free from sin?

Verse 11 tells us that the same Spirit that raised Jesus from the dead, the Holy Spirit, is in you through the New Birth and is quickening your mortal flesh. What does *quickening* mean?

The dictionary says it means *to make alive*. How awesome. The Holy Spirit is inside of you and comes on you to make you alive to God and dead to sin. How will you ever be able to mortify the deeds of your flesh? You will allow the power of God to quicken your flesh, so you can live the good life God has planned for you.

How much better can it get? While you simply enjoy the presence of God, the Holy Spirit works from the inside and from the outside to help you keep your flesh under. Keep in mind that this isn't any old power; this is the same power that raised Jesus from the dead and translated Him from one kingdom to another. It's that same power working inside and outside of you to transport you from the kingdom of darkness to the kingdom of light and empower you to live free from sin.

THE TRUTH MAKES YOU FREE

If you look over your life and think, *What's wrong with this picture? I've been continually struggling with sin*. Then it's time to turn all your attention to the Word of God because John 8:32 says, "You shall *know the truth, and the truth shall make you free*" (NKJV). God's Word doesn't just offer you a good suggestion here and there. It *makes* you free.

What's your part? Your part is to *know the truth*. What does that mean? Let me answer this way. Jesus is the Word made flesh to live among us (John 1:14). So when you know the Word of God, you will know the Son of God. John 8:36 says, "If the son therefore shall make you free, ye shall be free indeed." Jesus will set you free from the sins, the habits, and the junk that tries to shackle you.

Look at what Hebrews 4 tells us.

> **Hebrews 4:12 (NKJV)**
> 12 For the word of God is living and powerful, and sharper than any two-edged sword, piercing even to the division of soul and spirit, and of joints and marrow, and is a discerner of the thoughts and intents of the heart.

The Word of God is alive and powerful and sharper than even a double-edged sword. Only God's Word is able to divide between your soul and spirit or separate between what God is telling you and what your mind and emotions are telling you. Only the Word of God is powerful enough to help you separate your mental thoughts from your heart purposes.

What a powerful tool to help combat sin. The Word of God can perform surgery on us and help us identify attitudes, patterns and behaviors, so we can get out of the mess of sin and bad habits. God's Word can guide us out of sin into a life that's pleasing to the Lord.

Hebrews 1 says the Word of God is the power of God, and it's that power that you need in your life. Willpower is great, but a strong will is not enough to permanently deliver you from sin. Self-help programs are fine and good, but self-help programs are not enough. They may be a good start, but they won't get you to the finish line. You need God's Word abiding in your heart and demonstrated in your life, so the truth can *make you* everything you need to be.

WORDS MATTER

If I tell you that by making one small change, you can radically change your life for the better, would you make the change? Sure you would. That's why I'm telling you that the Bible says if you will control your mouth, you will control your entire body. If you'll line up your words with God's Word, your whole life can spin around and head in the right direction.

The truth is, if you talk like a sinner, sin is what you'll have. You shouldn't be saying things like, "I just cannot help myself." "I give up." "I never do anything right." "I've tried to defeat sin, but I keep failing." "I just cannot seem to say no." Do you read those sorts of statements in the Bible? No. Did Jesus talk like that? No. Then you shouldn't talk like that either.

Proverbs 18:21 says that the power of life and death are in the tongue, so what we're speaking matters a lot. In fact, James 3 tells us that if we will learn to control our tongues, we can control our whole body.

> **James 3:2-6 (NKJV)**
> 2 For we all stumble in many things. If anyone does not stumble in word, he is a perfect man, able also to bridle the whole body.
>
> 3 Indeed, we put bits in horses' mouths that they may obey us, and we turn their whole body.
>
> 4 Look also at ships: although they are so large and are driven by fierce winds, they are turned by a very small rudder wherever the pilot desires. 5 Even so the tongue is a little member and boasts great things. See how great a forest a little fire kindles!
>
> 6 And the tongue is a fire, a world of iniquity. The tongue is so set among our members that it defiles the whole body, and sets on fire the course of nature; and it is set on fire by hell.

Notice that verse 2 says that "if anyone does not stumble in word, he is . . . able also to bridle the whole body." Then notice how the scripture explains that the horse is controlled by a bit in its mouth, and the ship is controlled by a small rudder. Your tongue is just like that. Is it creating a world of iniquity for you or steering you to victory over sin?

Notice how The Amplified Bible translates this passage.

> **James 3:2-6 (AMP)**
> 2 For we all often stumble and fall and offend in many things. And if anyone does not offend in speech [never says the wrong things], he is a fully developed character and a perfect man, able to control his whole body and to curb his entire nature.
>
> 3 If we set bits in the horses' mouths to make them obey us, we can turn their whole bodies about.
>
> 4 Likewise, look at the ships: though they are so great and are driven by rough winds, they are steered by a very small rudder wherever the impulse of the helmsman determines.
>
> 5 Even so the tongue is a little member, and it can boast of great things. See how much wood or how great a forest a tiny spark can set ablaze!
>
> 6 And the tongue is a fire. [The tongue is a] world of wickedness set among our members, contaminating and depraving the whole body and setting on fire the wheel of birth (the cycle of man's nature), being itself ignited by hell (Gehenna).

We need to speak God's Word of freedom and victory over our lives daily, and watch God's Word bring freedom and victory to pass in our lives. The Bible says we are the righteousness of God in Christ Jesus (2 Corinthians 5:21). The Bible says that old things have passed away and all things are new (2 Corinthians 5:17). The Bible says we can do all things through Jesus Christ who strengthens us (Philippians 4:13). The Bible says we're the head and not the tail (Deuteronomy 28:13). The Bible says we have the mind of Christ (1 Corinthians 2:16). The Bible says that we triumph in every situation (2 Corinthians 2:14).

Revelation 12:11 says that we overcome the devil by the blood of the Lamb and the word of our testimony. Jesus has already done His part and provided His own blood to defeat the works of the devil and set us free. Now we must give the word of our testimony and declare and decree God's Word in our lives. That's how we overcome temptation, sin and everything else the devil throws our way.

FRIENDS

As a pastor I've watched people get born again, get filled with the Holy Spirit, get on fire for God and then two or three months later they're not around anymore. Why? They didn't learn from God's Word what it takes to live free.

Let's face it. People make mistakes. People will sin; nobody is perfect. But that's why we have 1 John 1:9 written to Christians. When we sin, we need to run to God and ask forgiveness, and He is faithful and just to forgive us. As Christians we need to be quick to ask for forgiveness, and we need to be quick to forgive.

We also need to help people who have sinned; sometimes we need to pick them up and restore them. Galatians 6:1 says, "Brethren, if a man is overtaken in any trespass, you who *are* spiritual restore such a one in a spirit of gentleness, considering yourself lest you also be tempted" (NKJV). The verse tells us to pick up people who have fallen into sin, restore them and leave them stronger. The verse also tells us to be wise about their temptation, not becoming tempted ourselves.

Along the same line, 1 Corinthians 15:33 says, "Be not deceived:

..." When the Bible says don't be deceived, it's like a neon light flashing to warn you: You will fall into a trap if you don't get the next part of this verse, which says "...evil communications corrupt good manners." The Amplified Bible puts it this way, "Do not be so deceived and misled! Evil companionships (communion, associations) corrupt and deprave good manners and morals and character."

You could be the most moral person around and be on fire for God, but if you hang around people who don't want to serve God and think sin is fun, it will take its toll on you. Of course we should reach out to help people who fall into sin, but these folks don't need to become our best buds.

Don't misunderstand me. I don't mean that we should have the attitude of "Don't touch me. I'm sanitized," but we cannot start hanging around sin in order to help them. We need to make sure that we pull folks up to our walk with God, not lower ourselves down to another's walk in the flesh.

If we see a Christian in sin, should we get out our sword and cut them down? Or should we say, "You big sinner"? No. We lovingly restore the person with the same nonjudgmental attitude Jesus had: "Neither do I condemn you, but go and sin no more."

On the other side of things, if you're a newer Christian, let me encourage you to make friends with believers who can help you grow strong. Find someone who's been walking with God for a while and let that person mentor you. I'm so glad that when I came into the church at 23 years of age and was delivered out of the life I was living, someone grabbed me and said, "Hey, let me show you the way."

When I first started pastoring, we had a small congregation of 15 to 20 people, and I bugged our people morning, noon and night. I was on the phone checking on them because I wanted to be there for them. I wanted to invest in their lives and do everything I could to help them grow, but these days it's no longer feasible if I also want to sleep. Nevertheless, the Bible says iron sharpens iron, so it's good to be around strong Christians who sharpen you. Be friends with people of like precious faith who will sharpen and encourage you.

The Bible is very clear that we all need to carefully choose our friends, and this also goes for parents who are responsible for knowing their children's friends. Don't let a child tell you that it's none of your business; God has made it your business, parents. Using caution picking the right friends isn't just good advice for our children; however, even as adults, we need to pick friends carefully.

CHAPTER 10
LIVING FREE

E arlier we read how Jesus ministered to the woman in John 8 who had sinned. While everyone else around the woman judged her and condemned her to death, Jesus had a whole different attitude. He didn't condone her sin, but neither did He condemn her. He told the woman, "Go and sin no more."

These are life-changing words Jesus spoke. Even more amazing is the God-given power behind these words to help you and me do the same. Jesus was telling the woman who had sinned—and all of us today—that it's possible to go and sin no more.

Jesus would tell you today that you can break free, stay free and live free from sin.

If you've received Jesus as your Savior, you're not like everyone else walking around on this earth. In the split second you were born again, something different happened on the inside of you. You were filled with God Himself, and the more you allow what's on the inside to show up on the outside, you will walk differently, talk differently, act differently, believe differently and altogether be different.

The devil tries to shackle us to our past lives of sin. But it's too late. We've exposed his trickery and deceit with the truth of God's Word. God's Word tells us that Jesus defeated sin on the cross 2,000 years ago. Jesus removed our sin; His blood washed it away. Jesus already raised us to be seated next to Him in heavenly places.

Now the choice is yours. All that's left is for you to receive the redemption Jesus purchased for you and walk in it. We're no longer just sinners saved by grace; we're no longer shackled by sin. We're sons and daughters of God and joint heirs with Jesus and no devil in hell can stop us from taking our place so it's time to act like it.

Jesus came to earth to show us how to live, and it's time we follow His example. Jesus knew who He was. Jesus knew that He had power over the devil and sin. Jesus knew He had dominion in this earth. When He spoke to storms, they calmed. When He spoke to fevers, they broke.

Jesus also gave us power. Luke 10:19 says, "Behold, I give you the authority…over all the power of the enemy.…" Now He expects us to exert dominion in the world around us. He expects us declare and decree His Word. He expects the power of the Holy Spirit to demonstrate His Word through us. And He expects that we exert dominion in our own minds and bodies.

After all, as a Christian you have a new nature on the inside of you. You have put on new clothes. You are the temple of the Holy Spirit, and you walk in the Spirit. You have received the free gift of righteousness. You are armed with the Word of God as your weapon, and you're guided through life by the Holy Spirit. God has given you every supernatural tool needed to win over sin.

SUPERNATURAL RESTORATION

God cares so much about His children that He wants us to do more than conquer sin; He wants us to recover what sin has stolen. God restored the children of Israel as they came out of Egypt. He restored David. He restored the prodigal son. And God will restore you.

When the children of Israel came up out of Egypt, which was a type of sin, they recovered all that God had long before promised Abraham, Isaac and Jacob in His covenant with them. Through miraculous intervention, God brought the Israelites out of slavery. They could have left with nothing—except they had a covenant that was everything. The Bible says that God brought them out with silver and gold and not one sick or feeble person was among them. Just as God delivered the Israelites from bondage and restored their health and wealth and all the enemy had stolen, He stands ready to do the same for you right now!

Through this Old Testament account, God restored His children and showed us what redemption would look like at the same time. He showed them the goodness of God and promised to lead them to the land of promise. He promised to restore their land to them because it belonged to them; it still does today. Unfortunately, a great number of the Israelites got their eyes off the promise and ended up in the wilderness for 40 years. Those who doubted never saw the Promised Land at all, but those who believed did.

What is your Promised Land?

Maybe your Promised Land looks impossible to you at the moment; maybe the enemies look too big like they did in the eyes of many Israelites. But God's Word is full of great and precious promises that enable you to take hold of every godly thing you need or want. These blessings are not for when you get to heaven; they are available in the here and now.

Don't let the same thing happen to you that happened to the Israelites. Don't get bogged down in doubt and unbelief. Make up your mind that you will enjoy everything God has promised you, and God will restore back to you anything sin has stolen.

"Yeah, but, how can God restore anything to me? I got myself into trouble. Sin was my fault." I understand that, and God does, too. But Psalm 107:20 says God will deliver us from *all our destructions*, so hold on to the promise of restoration.

In 1 Samuel 30, King David and his men returned to Ziklag from battle and the place was burned down. The women, the children and all their possessions were gone. Things looked bleak all around.

> **1 Samuel 30:2-4**
> 2 [The enemy] had taken the women captives, that were therein: they slew not any, either great or small, but carried them away, and went on their way.
>
> 3 So David and his men came to the city, and, behold, it was burned with fire; and their wives, and their sons, and their daughters, were taken captives.
>
> 4 Then David and the people that were with him lifted up their voice and wept, until they had no more power to weep.

Maybe you have experienced this kind of devastation in life where all you could do was weep. Maybe you have felt like the wind was knocked out of you. The verse below says there's only one thing to do at a time like that.

> **1 Samuel 30:6**
> 6 And David was greatly distressed; for the people spake of stoning him, because the soul of all the people was grieved, every man for his sons and for his daughters: but David encouraged himself in the Lord his God.

David had been the hero and all was well, but then things went from bad to worse. The people talked of stoning David, their once great leader. So what did David do when it looked like things couldn't get any worse? Verse 6 says *"...David encouraged himself in the LORD his God."*

When it feels like you were punched in the stomach and grieving over mistakes gone by, you've got to make up your mind to quit grieving and encourage yourself in the Lord. Maybe your sins and bad choices stole from you. Maybe temptation and sin caused you to wreck your whole life or another's. Maybe you lost your spouse or your job or your whole family. Maybe you lost your reputation or years of enjoying life. It doesn't matter. God can still restore what you've lost if you will trust Him and follow Him.

Things might look bad—family situations, health situations, financial situations and even relationships—but you've got to get up and encourage yourself in the Lord. It's nice when other people pick up the phone and encourage you, but you cannot always depend on them. David had to grab himself by what I like to call the nape of the neck and say, "Soul, you will encourage yourself. Why are you so disquieted within me; you will yet praise God" (Psalm 42:5).

You also need to encourage yourself.

God has brought you from where you were to here, and He's not finished yet.

The temptation and sin or devastation you have faced was sent by the devil to destroy you, but you're still standing. Restoration may look impossible, but with God nothing is impossible. And that's why you can encourage yourself and be encouraged.

In verses 7 and 8, we read how David decided that he needed to ask God for advice, which is always a good idea.

1 Samuel 30:7-8
7 And David said to Abiathar the priest,

> Ahimelech's son, I pray thee, bring me hither the ephod. And Abiathar brought thither the ephod to David.
>
> 8 And David enquired at the Lord, saying, Shall I pursue after this troop? Shall I overtake them? And he answered him, Pursue: for thou shalt surely overtake them, and without fail recover all.

David went before the Lord and asked, "Shall I go after this army; what shall I do? What's the game plan?" That was wise of David because every battle we face is not the same. The Word of God will always win, but you and I still need to be led by the Spirit of God. There were times that David went after the enemy, and there were other times when he needed to stand still and see the salvation of the Lord.

What did God tell David to do? Pursue. What do you suppose God is telling you to do? Pursue.

David didn't sit by silently, and he didn't sit by singing, "Kumbaya, my Lord, kumbaya." No, he asked the Lord what to do and then took off recovering what had been stolen from him. I believe the Lord is telling you the same thing. Don't wait for the devil to attack you again with temptation or sin. Pursue. Pursue a new place in God. Pursue a sin-free life. Pursue restoration of what sin stole from you.

Be strong in the Lord every day. Be blessed in the Lord every day. The Bible says the just shall live by faith, so put faith to work in your life and continually speak God's Word over every area of your life. If you do, you won't have to fight so many adversaries all the time, and the ones that do show up won't be such a big deal to overcome.

Restoration of all things won't happen automatically in your life. "Well, if it's God's will for me, it will just happen. If it's not God's will, then it just won't," someone might say. That's not true, and that's not Bible. The will of God is not automatically done in this life. The Bible says that it is God's will for everyone to be saved, and God is not willing that any perish. But is everyone you know saved? No. Every day people in sin meet eternity.

Then who determines if the will of God is done in your life? Your spouse? Your pastor? No. The Holy Ghost can't even make it happen.

The choice is yours.

The Word of God and the Spirit of God will guide you into all truth and empower you to walk in it, but you must do the walking.

"But, Pastor, how do I know it's God's will for things to be restored to me?" John 10:10 says the devil comes to steal, kill and destroy, but Jesus comes to give abundant life. God sent Jesus to give a full, amazing life to all who believe on Him. All through the Epistles, the Word makes it clear that God wants good things for us.

Remember in the New Testament how God restored the prodigal son? Luke 15 tells the story of the young man who squandered all he had with prodigal or wild living. When he came to himself and there was famine in the land, he decided to return home. Then verse 21 says the son said to his father, "'Father, I have sinned against heaven and in your sight, and am no longer worthy to be called your son'" (NKJV).

But the father lovingly and compassionately received his son. Sonship was restored. Father and son were reunited. The family was reunited. With a ring on his finger, the son got his authority back, and he got his wealth back because God is the restorer.

People who have sinned against the heavenly Father often have the same attitude the prodigal son had. "I don't deserve anything," they say. And they're right. They don't. But the father in Luke 15 looked past what the son deserved, and your heavenly Father looks past what you deserve.

God wants to restore you in every area of life, and the best evidence of all is found in Jesus' own words below.

> **Luke 4:18-19 (NKJV)**
> 18 The Spirit of the LORD *is* upon Me, Because He has anointed Me To preach the gospel to the poor; He has sent Me to heal the brokenhearted, To proclaim liberty to the captives, And recovery of sight to the blind, To set at liberty those who are oppressed;
>
> 19 To proclaim the acceptable year of the Lord.

What is the *acceptable year of the Lord* referred to in verse 19? It is the Jubilee found in Leviticus 25.

> **Leviticus 25:9-10, 13 (NKJV)**
> 9 Then you shall cause the trumpet of the Jubilee to sound on the tenth day of the seventh month; on the Day of Atonement you shall make the trumpet to sound throughout all your land.
>
> 10 And you shall consecrate the fiftieth year, and proclaim liberty throughout all the land to all its inhabitants. It shall be a Jubilee for you; and each of you shall return to his possession, and each of you shall return to his family.
>
> 13 'In this Year of Jubilee, each of you shall return to his possession.

On the day of atonement the trumpet of Jubilee would sound throughout the land, and people would return to their possessions and their families. The Bible goes on to say that every 50 years the trumpet would sound and the people would shout out, "Jubilee! Jubilee!"

If family members were separated because of slavery or compelled to sell possessions through poverty, they would be restored during Jubilee. Think about it. If someone took a house, it would be restored when the Jubilee trumpet sounded. You could knock on a door and say, "Jubilee, give my family back. OK, give my house back." "Excuse me, those cabinets, those are mine. That bed, that's mine. You may leave now. Jubilee! Did you hear the trumpet?"

So what did Jesus mean in Luke 4:19 when He said He was here to preach the acceptable year of the Lord? Jesus was telling every one of us that *He is our Jubilee*. When Jesus paid the ultimate price for us on the cross, atonement came to us throughout the land once and for all. Now it's Jubilee every day for us—every single day.

It's Jubilee for *you*.

Pursue what you've lost because God is in the restoration business. Jesus said He Himself preached the acceptable year of the Lord, and it's time to recover all you've lost. It doesn't matter what you lost or how you lost it; God can return it. Even if you deserved to lose something, God wants to bring restoration to you. Jesus came to set us free wherever we need to be set free and restore whatever we've lost.

Maybe you were married and got divorced and both of you are now remarried. Does that mean you should go back to your first wife? No. God won't rearrange the lives of four people because you have figured out that you made a mistake. But God can restore the marriage you are in now.

Maybe you've been married three times and you just got born again and filled with the Holy Ghost; maybe now for the first time things are going well. Maybe you're thinking, *Oh, I really messed up. I better go back.* No. In a situation like that, you cannot go back; but God will make the marriage you are in now the best marriage it could possibly be. In other words, God won't necessarily restore a person back to you, but He'll restore marriage to you. He'll restore family to you.

Maybe you didn't do well in raising your children when they were young. It's never too late. I've watched God rearrange lives and restore families where it appeared impossible.

Maybe you feel like drugs and alcohol have stolen years of your life. Joel 2:25 says God will restore the years to you that the locusts have eaten. It doesn't matter how much time has passed. God has a way of restoring things.

Think of the Shunammite woman in 2 Kings 4 who helped the prophet Elisha. Remember her son had died, and Elisha raised him from the dead. Then later in 2 Kings 8, the prophet told the woman that a famine was coming, so she left her land and traveled to the land of the Philistines.

What happened? Seven years later, after the famine, she returned to her homeland and was petitioning the king to get her land back. God positioned her at the right place with her son while the prophet's assistant, Gehazi, was telling the king everything Elisha was doing and how he raised the boy from the dead.

When the king realized the miracle that had occurred with the boy, he immediately restored the woman's land to her. And because God is in the restoration business, he moved on the king to also give the woman all the money that was made off the land during the time she was away.

"Yeah, but, she didn't deserve it. That wasn't right." Favor isn't fair. If you don't want to walk in favor, I'll take yours. Favor is better than fair, and the righteous are encompassed about with favor.

God restored the Israelites to their Promised Land. God restored David. God restored the prodigal son. God restored the Shunammite woman. And God will restore you. I don't know what you've lost, but God does, and He will restore it to you.

RUN YOUR RACE

God wants you free and restored in every area of life. God's plan for you is a happily ever after for your whole family. Yet, if we intend to finish strong, we must realize that we're not running in a sprint; we're running in a marathon.

We need to determine right now to walk in the divine nature we've been given from now until we go to heaven or Jesus returns. We want to make it to the end and hear, "Well done, good and faithful servant," and walking free of sin is a big part of it.

Hebrews 12 tells us in the following verses what we must do to focus on running and winning our race.

> **Hebrews 12:1-2**
> 1 Therefore we also, since we are surrounded by so great a cloud of witnesses, let us lay aside every weight, and the sin which so easily ensnares us, and let us run with endurance the race that is set before us,
> 2 looking unto Jesus, the author and finisher of our faith, who for the joy that was set before Him endured the cross, despising the shame, and has sat down at the right hand of the throne of God.

As heaven cheers us on, each of us has a race to run, and to run well, we must lay aside weights and sins that ensnare us. Why? So we can run with endurance and cross the finish line.

Imagine a marathon runner in a race all lined up at the starting line. The gun fires, but he or she can hardly make it down the lane because he or she is dragging 25-pound weights, 100-pound weights, barbells, dumbbells and even tin cans. Whether you've ever been a runner or an athlete or not, it's pretty easy to figure out that extra weight will make you slow and ineffective in your race.

With that in mind, look at the same verses in The Amplified Bible.

> **Hebrews 12:1-2 (AMP)**
> 1 Therefore then, since we are surrounded by so great a cloud of witnesses [who have borne testimony to the Truth], let us strip off and throw aside every encumbrance (unnecessary weight) and that sin which so readily (deftly and cleverly) clings to and entangles us, and let us run with patient endurance and steady and active persistence the appointed course of the race that is set before us,
>
> 2 Looking away [from all that will distract] to Jesus, Who is the Leader and the Source of our faith [giving the first incentive for our belief] and is also its Finisher [bringing it to maturity and perfection]. He, for the joy [of obtaining the prize] that was set before Him, endured the cross, despising and ignoring the shame, and is now seated at the right hand of the throne of God.

I like the strong language in The Amplified version. Let us strip off and throw aside every weight and the sin that so readily clings to and entangles us. Isn't that just the way sin feels? Sin traps and entangles us. It cleverly clings to us and pushes our buttons. Worse yet, it tangles up our feet while we try to run.

The New Testament in Modern English translation puts it this way, "…Strip off everything that hinders us, as well as the sin which dogs our feet, and let us run the race that we have to run with patience, our eyes fixed on Jesus the source and the goal of our faith." If you're reading this book, I know you've felt at times that sin dogs your feet and nips at your heels.

But fix your eyes on Jesus, the source and the goal of your faith.

If you look to Jesus, He will be the author and finisher of your faith. Jesus will help you finish strong.

RECEIVING A CROWN

Yet, do you realize that your finish line is not heaven? As a believer, your finish line is the judgment seat of Christ. That's where you will receive your reward for the things you have done on the earth, and hopefully, that's where Jesus will say to you, "Well done, good and faithful servant." Unfortunately, Jesus won't be able to say that to everybody. Every born-again individual will spend eternity in heaven, but that doesn't necessarily mean he or she will hear, "Well done!"

Years ago I began to think about this a lot. I would think about how the Lord had given me so much. He saved me. He delivered me. He healed me and provided for me financially. He gave me a great life. God has done so many things for me, and I'm grateful to Him. Not only *should* I obey Him, but also I *want* to obey Him. With all my heart, I want to please Him.

But besides your love, there is really only one thing He wants from you and me. There is only one thing that you and I will have for all of eternity to give back to Him: obedience.

For example, there are lots of things we need to do. We need to tithe. We need to give offerings. We need to help the poor. We need to fulfill the Great Commission. We need to study God's Word. We need to help in the church. But really, all those things can be wrapped up in one word: obedience.

You see, when I stand in front of Him all by myself at the judgment seat of Christ—eyeball to eyeball—He will ask me one question. The big question will be: Did you do what I asked you to do on the earth? At that point, I'll have one of two choices. I'll either say "Yes!" or "Lord, let me tell You the reasons why I couldn't obey."

I believe He'll put up His hand and say, "Not now! I don't want to hear it."

So I desperately want to be able to say, "Yes, Lord!"

Don't you?

The Bible tells us that Jesus will give crowns to those of us who have obeyed Him, and there will be a great worship service in heaven. Notice I said those of us who have crowns because I included myself. I've made up my mind that I will obey Him, and I will receive one of those crowns. Have you made up your mind?

"Oh, Pastor, do you think I'll get a crown some day?" Let me ask you this. Is obeying Jesus the most important thing in your life? If you've answered yes, then I believe you will receive a crown one day. That means you'll be among those who have obeyed, and you will have the privilege of removing your crown and laying it as His feet. Giving Jesus your crown because you obeyed while on the earth will be the best thing you do throughout all eternity.

Sadly, I've noticed there are some people who have served God, but they walked away from Him. Maybe they didn't get their prayers answered. Maybe they didn't really understand faith. Maybe they didn't obtain their healing or maybe a lot of different scenarios. More often than not, however, they are people who no longer serve God because they fell in to sin at some point.

Maybe they're in what we call a backslidden condition, where they were born again and walking with God but literally slipped backward. Or maybe the person was never really born again; his or her life was never really transformed.

I know one thing. If you're reading this book, then you love God and want to serve Him, and as you've read chapter after chapter you've become empowered with the truth that's able to make you free. So decide to run your race and strive for your crown.

Here's what the apostle Paul tells us:

> **1 Corinthians 9:24-27**
> 24 Know ye not that they which run in a race run all, but one receiveth the prize? So run, that ye may obtain.
>
> 25 And every man that striveth for the mastery is temperate in all things. Now they do it to obtain a corruptible crown; but we an incorruptible.
>
> 26 I therefore so run, not as uncertainly; so fight I, not as one that beateth the air:
>
> 27 But I keep under my body, and bring it into subjection: lest that by any means, when I have preached to others, I myself should be a castaway.

What's the prize that the apostle Paul is talking about? He's talking about your crown, the reward you receive at the end of your race. He says the man or woman who strives for the mastery is temperate in all things. The word *temperate* means to control your flesh and not overdo things. Does the scripture say in how many things we are to be temperate? It says in *all things*.

Let me give you an example from a number of years ago. We had an athlete in our church who was a state champion wrestler. Even though he was only in the ninth grade at the time, no one would have messed with him. Do you know why? The boy trained and lifted weights; he was strong, and he had muscles. He ate right and worked hard because he was training for a title.

Likewise, you and I are also in training. We're in the event of our lives, and we're competing for an incorruptible crown. We also need to lift off weights and develop our faith muscles. We need to eat the right spiritual food and work hard. We need to renew our minds and keep our bodies under control so we can win our race.

That's why Paul likened his life to a race and said of himself:

> **1 Corinthians 9:25-27 (AMP)**
> 25 Now every athlete who goes into training conducts himself temperately and restricts himself in all things. They do it to win a wreath that will soon wither, but we [do it to receive a crown of eternal blessedness] that cannot wither.
>
> 26 Therefore I do not run uncertainly (without definite aim). I do not box like one beating the air and striking without an adversary.
>
> 27 But [like a boxer] I buffet my body [handle it roughly, discipline it by hardships] and subdue it, for fear that after proclaiming to others the Gospel and things pertaining to it, I myself should become unfit [not stand the test, be unapproved and rejected as a counterfeit].

Paul said he's determined. Paul said he really fights. He said that he is the sternest master of his body. Notice that it did not say that Paul asked God to control his body. Paul did not ask a friend to keep his body under. He did not ask Barnabus to help him out. He did not ask Cornelius to discipline his body.

A lot of people pray and pray for God to help them deal with sin and temptation. A lot of people ask friends for help. Some people try to help their friends keep their bodies under, and you've got to wonder how long they will be friends. Some people use the biggest excuse of all and say, "I couldn't help myself. The devil made me do it." Friend, those are all lies—every one of them.

You are responsible for *you*.

Too often Christians like to blame the devil and evil spirits for things that are just plain old undisciplined flesh. I've heard it over and over, "My husband gets so angry sometimes. He must be possessed with a demon." Most likely he's not. Most likely your husband just refuses to control his flesh. Let's give equal opportunity here. I've had husbands say to me, "My wife has a demon. I just know it. She's so mean she's evil." Most likely she doesn't. Most likely your wife just refuses to control her flesh.

Paul shared the secret to a successful Christian life when he said, "I keep my body under and bring it into subjection." This is a man who wrote two-thirds of the New Testament and took the gospel of Jesus Christ pretty much around the known world in his day. And he said keeping the body under—ruling over sin—is how to win the prize and not be a castaway.

No one reading this book wants to be a castaway. We want to be overcomers. We want to finish our course. We want to complete our race. So let's win the prize and receive the crown. Let's leave sin behind and run our race no longer shackled by sin.

A PRAYER TO OVERCOME SIN

The first step toward overcoming sin is to receive Jesus as your Lord and Savior. It will change you from the inside out and enable you to take hold of supernatural tools and help you to get free, stay free and live free from sin. It all begins by praying this simple prayer aloud:

> Dear heavenly Father: Your Word says, "Whosoever shall call on the name of the Lord shall be saved" (Acts 2:21). I call on You right now.
>
> The Bible also says if I confess with my mouth that Jesus is Lord and believe in my heart that You have raised Him from the dead, I shall be saved (Romans 10:9-10). I make that choice now.
>
> Jesus, I believe in You. I believe in my heart and confess with my mouth that You died on the cross for my sins and that You were raised from the dead. I ask You to be my Lord and Savior. Thank You for forgiving me of all my sins. I believe I'm now a new creation in You. Old things have passed away; all things have become new in Jesus' name (2 Corinthians 5:17). Amen.

If you prayed this prayer today, please share the good news with us!
Cornerstone Word of Life Church
(256) 461-7055 or office@cwol.org

ENDNOTES

CHAPTER 3

Based on a definition from James Strong, Greek Dictionary of the New Testament in *Strong's Exhaustive Concordance of the Bible* (Nashville: Thomas Nelson, 1984), as found in PC Study Bible v.5.

Based on a definition from The Livingston Corporation, Life Application New Testament Commentary(Town: Tyndale House Publishers, Inc.,), as found at in WordSearch 8 at WORDsearchbible.com.

Based on a definition from W.E Vine, V*ine's Expository Dictionary of the Old & New Testament Words* (Nashville: Thomas Nelson, 1984), as found in PC Study Bible v.5.

CHAPTER 5

Rick Renner, *Sparkling Gems from the Greek*, (Tulsa, Oklahoma: Teach All Nations, A Division of Rick Renner Ministries, 2003), 946.

CHAPTER 6

Rick Renner, *Sparkling Gems from the Greek*, (Tulsa, Oklahoma: Teach All Nations, A Division of Rick Renner Ministries, 2003), 490.

CHAPTER 8

Rick Renner, *Dressed to Kill*, (Tulsa, Oklahoma: Teach All Nations, A Division of Rick Renner Ministries, 2003), 131-132.

www.ingramcontent.com/pod-product-compliance
Lightning Source LLC
Chambersburg PA
CBHW061653040426
42446CB00010B/1712